D0530634

One Kind of Everything

One Kind of Everything

Poem and Person in Contemporary America

DAN CHIASSON

The University of Chicago Press ❋ *Chicago and London*

DAN CHIASSON is visiting assistant professor of English at Wellesley College. He is the author of two books of poems, *Natural History* (2005) and *The Afterlife of Objects* (2002), the latter published by the University of Chicago Press.

The University of Chicago Press, Chicago 60637
The University of Chicago Press, Ltd., London
© 2007 by The University of Chicago
All rights reserved. Published 2007
Printed in the United States of America
16 15 14 13 12 11 10 09 08 07   1 2 3 4 5
ISBN-13: 978-0-226-10381-5 (cloth)
ISBN-10: 0-226-10381-1 (cloth)
"Why I Am Not a Painter," from *Collected Poems* by Frank O'Hara, copyright © 1971 by Maureen Granville-Smith, Administratrix of the Estate of Frank O' Hara. Used by permission of Alfred A. Knopf, a division of Random House, Inc.

Library of Congress Cataloging-in-Publication Data
Chiasson, Dan.
    One kind of everything : poem and person in contemporary America / Dan Chiasson.
        p.   cm.
    Includes index.
    ISBN-13: 978-0-226-10381-5 (cloth : alk. paper)
    ISBN-10: 0-226-10381-1 (cloth : alk. paper)
        1. American poetry—20th century—History and criticism.   2. Autobiography in literature.   3. Self in literature.   I. Title.

PS323.5 .C485 2006
811'.509353—dc22
                                                2006016654

♾ The paper used in this publication meets the minimum requirements of the American National Standard for Information Sciences—Permanence of Paper for Printed Library Materials, ANSI Z39.48-1992.

Contents

Acknowledgments

This work depended on the support and counsel of many people, not all of them singled out here. I am particularly grateful to my teachers: Philip Fisher, Elisa New, William Pritchard, Peter Sacks, Elaine Scarry, and above all Helen Vendler.

I have been blessed with many friends who are also themselves poets and readers of poetry, some of whom commented directly on this project. Many thanks to Frank Bidart, William Cain, Peter Campion, Jeffrey Dolven, David Ferry, Forrest Gander, Louise Glück, Jorie Graham, Desales Harrison, Jamaica Kincaid, Nicholas Lolordo, Peter Manning, Timothy Peltason, Kathleen Peterson, Robert Pinsky, Jeffrey Posternak, Lawrence Rosenwald, Margery Sabin, Susan Sheckel, Tom Sleigh, and Douglas Trevor. This work benefited greatly from the editorial counsel of Richard Poirier at *Raritan*, Sven Birkerts and Bill Pierce at *Agni*, and, at the Association of Literary Scholars and Critics, Christopher Ricks and Rosanna Warren. Thanks also to those periodicals in which earlier versions of some chapters previously appeared: the chapter on Robert Lowell in "Reading 'Blizzard in Cambridge,'" *Salmagundi*, nos. 141–42 (2004), pp. 156–58; the chapter on Elizabeth Bishop's "Crusoe in England" first appeared in *Agni* 62, under the title "One Kind of Everything"; and portions of the chapter on Frank Bidart appeared under the title "Presence: Frank Bidart," *Raritan* 20, no. 4 (2001): 117–38.

I would like to thank my editor at the University of Chicago Press, Randolph Petilos, and my copy editor there, Yvonne Zipter.

My life is immeasurably enriched by my wife Annie Adams and our son, Louis. This book is dedicated to my mother, without whom I would not have had the freedom to read poetry in the first place.

Introduction:
"One Kind of Everything"

Canting, Recanting

This is a book about the relationship between fact and figure in American poetry. Poetic figuration (and the imaginative activity it emblematizes) has come to seem, to many who have considered the matter, either afactual or explicitly antifactual, the mark of renunciation and transcendence in the face of mere fact. The particular class of "autobiographical" facts I will discuss in these pages seem especially mundane, which is to say, especially subject to triumphant transcendence (and erasure) by the imagination. This bias against autobiography seems, for reasons I will discuss, particularly American or, to be more precise, particularly Americanist. The primary sponsors of this bias would seem to be Ralph Waldo Emerson and Walt Whitman, who (in texts like Emerson's "The Poet" and Whitman's 1855 preface to *Leaves of Grass*) expounded a notion of poetic accomplishment "commensurate" (in Whitman's phrase) with the large reality of the American aggregate.

Of course both Emerson and Whitman were artists of profound individual impress and consequence, and each of them

have been read as articulating a deep rationale for American autobiography. Near the beginning of her study of American poetry,
The Line's Eye, for example, Elisa New describes the changes
undergone by Ralph Waldo Emerson in the years following his
son Waldo's death, changes that issued in his great essay "Experience." New describes an Emerson whose idealism, even though
recently and persuasively minted in "Nature," could not account
for the brute fact of a five-year-old's death from pneumonia.
From then on, New argues, "Nature would be what happened
to Waldo": "While 'Nature' had promised Americans breadths
of possession commensurate with their scope of imagination,
'Experience' shrinks the eye's empire to a swimming mote. 'Experience' amounts to Emerson's personal abrogation and our
literature's most moving recanting of what Harold Bloom has
called the 'American Sublime'" (New 4). For New's Emerson,
Waldo's death seemed suddenly and brutally to negate not only
the claims for the imagination but the ability, the desire, to make
such claims. The imagination would henceforth be not transcendent but relational, not original and transformative but radically
contingent on "what happened," following from "what happened
to Waldo." Though the Emerson passage is familiar, I will quote
it now in full. "In the death of my son, now more than two years
ago," he writes:

> I seem to have lost a beautiful estate,—no more. I cannot get it
> nearer to me. If tomorrow I should be informed of the bankruptcy
> of my principal debtors, the loss of my property would be a great
> inconvenience to me, perhaps, for many years; but it would leave me
> as it found me,—neither better nor worse. So is it with this calamity:
> it does not touch me: some thing which I fancied was a part of me,
> which could not be torn away without tearing me, nor enlarged with-
> out enriching me, falls off from me, and leaves no scar. It was cadu-
> cous. I grieve that grief can teach me nothing, nor carry me one step
> into real nature. (Emerson 205)

The passage, and the essay at large, evinces Emerson's "nausea and
dismay at the yawning gap between actual and ideal experience,"
as Lawrence Buell has written (Buell 126). Emerson's turn away

from the ideal and toward the actual, away from the imagination as transcendent and toward the imagination as relational, fixed on objects not of its making, defined by such objects, is simultaneously a turn toward autobiography. According to Buell and New, Emerson's grief establishes a new scale of the personal and near-at-hand, where distance, panorama, and vista (once valorized) now seem annihilating. The lament here is not "I cannot extend myself into the world" but, rather, "I cannot get it nearer to me." Cannot get it nearer, that is, even by figuration: Emerson's striking, even transgressive, choice of analogies is meant to fail both from his point of view and ours, its failure indicating the torrential grief it cannot fully embody. This event will not be transformed by the imagination; it will not serve as an imaginative means or vehicle "to carry me one step into mere nature."

I want to begin with this, perhaps the most important autobiographical disclosure in our literature, because I believe it has so much to tell us, still, about the literary uses of autobiography. In Emerson we see the earliest suggestion that the failure of the imagination and autobiography are causally connected. The recalcitrance of Waldo's death within the imagination, its resistance to transformation, forces what New calls Emerson's "recanting" of "the American Sublime." We think of poetic imagination as moving forward, on an extravagant errand. The sudden swerve, the unexpected delay, the colorful or threatening distraction—these are the phenomena that characterize the poetic imagination. But to "recant" is to call imagination back, to say "your work is here, not in some ineffable elsewhere." The gravity of the here and now, its need for imaginative tending, is something many writers besides Emerson have described, but for Emerson this sudden density of self must come as a particular shock—given his classic description, in "Nature," of the poet's "transparency." To be a self, Emerson implies here, is to be what Stevens said: "too dumbly in my being pent" (Stevens 96). Emerson would seem to inaugurate the use of remorse and its speech act, "recanting," as an imaginative occasion.

But this occasion for "recanting" is also, to develop the pun that New's term suggests, an occasion for "canting." Whatever else "Experience" is, it is one of the great testaments of Emerson's imagination, a gorgeous song about the futility of song. It opens up a new topic for American literature, the refusal to imagine. (The exquisitely, sublimely imagined refusal to imagine: there is play in the twined refusals and indulgences in Emerson's work, a play of giving and withholding that many "austere" American writers following Emerson are deaf to.) And indeed, many of Emerson's critics—I am thinking of Harold Bloom and Richard Poirier—suggest that, far more than "The Poet," "Experience" is Emerson's proscriptive, or perhaps preemptive, poetics. For Poirier, its self-consuming style invokes a proto-pragmatist poetics where figuration compensates for linguistic slippage, and Jamesian "vagueness" predominates: his Emersonian poets are Stein, Stevens, and Frost. For Bloom, the essay invokes a poetics of Shakespearean fullness, contradictoriness, and negative capability.

I do not mean to say that poets who write autobiography inevitably do so as a way of recanting earlier boasts; nor do I mean to equate "autobiography" and "trauma"—though the two have been linked, and for interesting reasons. What I want to suggest is an invigorating relationship between autobiography and figuration, a relationship this book explores in great detail. For me the "recanting" of Emerson's idealism cannot be separated from his new sense of autobiographical fact as final, nonnegotiable, and fixed. It is therefore possible to describe autobiography in Emersonian terms, indeed to see autobiographical fact as one of the crucial matters for American poetry in its Emersonian understanding of itself. To do so helps us see why American poetry's engagement with autobiographical fact has been such an immensely charged issue, from Whitman forward. One thing a person does when writing about the "actual," to employ Buell's term, is acknowledge its distance from the ideal—and, furthermore, to do so within a traceable Emersonian logic of regret and remorse.

And yet, though autobiography has been seen as an imaginative concession, a reliance on the lower gifts, the minor orders of inspiration, this view does not seem to me present in "Experience." Emerson's own candor is, there, quickly absorbed in figuration—in the image of a foreclosed "beautiful estate," far from any actual or objective "fact" about his grief, and in the later, bolder figures, a catalog of figures for, and in place of, the fact of Waldo's death: "[This calamity] does not touch me; something which I fancied was a part of me, which could not be torn away without tearing me nor enlarged without enriching me, falls off from me and leaves no scar. It was caduceus. . . . The Indian that was laid under a curse that the wind should not blow on him, nor water flow to him, nor fire burn him, is a type of us all. The dearest events are summer rain, and we the Para coats that shed every drop." The death of a child turns us into creditors, or fabric, or "the Indian" or a Para coat—turns us, that is, into trope. Far from foreclosing further imaginative acts, this grief opens us to the possibility of figurative objectification (itself allegorized by the flamboyant, "figurative" list). The sadness that underscores "Experience" also, by the way, sponsors the massive imaginative triumph represented by "Experience." There is no way to read this essay, Emerson's boldest, except by passing through the portal of Emerson's renunciation of imaginative boldness.

As "Experience" suggests and as the American confessional poets will demonstrate, the moment of confession cannot be other than theatrical, staged within the conventions, the props, of lyric poetry. Intimacy, candor, disclosure—all the qualities we associate with confession are the effects of artifice, deliberately wrought. Whitman often makes this notion explicit, as in the sublime diminuendo section 6 of "Crossing Brooklyn Ferry" where a list of his vices ("It is not upon you the dark patches fall . . .") becomes a meditation on the inevitability of roles and role-playing in emotional life:

> [I] lived the same life with the rest, the same old laughing,
>   gnawing, sleeping,
> Play'd the part that still looks back on the actor or actress,
> The same old role, the role that is what we make it, as great as we
>   like,
> Or as small as we like, or both great and small.
>
> (*Leaves* 311)

"Agonies are one of my changes of garments," he says elsewhere, in "Song of Myself." Read the usual way, this comment dismisses "agonies" as a sufficient subject for poems, denying them any special status above other kinds of experiences. Read another way, though, Whitman is boldly comparing "agonies" to costumes we change when the scene or act calls for a change. Of course Emerson was not playing a role when he mourned his son's death; but Whitman's authorial "I" is by nature theatrical, draped, like Emerson's, in figure, and its performance of intimacy (it's least obviously artificial, most "sincere" role) is likely to seem finally its most stunning performance.

Yet paradoxically, if autobiography can be the source for and inspiration of trope, one of its claims is to be free of, beyond, tropes. "From then on," writes New of Emerson, "Nature would be what happened to Waldo." The phrase "what happened" is one of the few that still indicates a place outside of rhetoric and trope, in an intellectual culture that has consigned virtually everything else one says to the status of "things one says." When we ask someone "what happened" we expect the unadorned, the true—not the "true"—account. But the unrhetorical, the un-troped, is of tremendous use in the making of poems, perhaps our most radiantly troped and rhetorical literary genre. As an example of the power of "what happened" within rhetoric, we need only remember the presence of Waldo's death in "Experience" (and, indeed, in the present work) or, in T. S. Eliot's letter to John Hayward, the presence of "some acute personal reminiscence." Writing on "Little Gidding," Eliot remarks: "The defect of the whole poem, I feel, is the lack of some acute personal reminiscence (never to be explicated, of course, but to give power well beneath the surface)" (Gardner 67). The "reminiscence" Eliot anticipates might well be titled *Life Studies*—by Robert Lowell. We have been trained to recognize the aesthetic value of suppression, perhaps of repression, where anecdote, gossip, disclosure, and complaint are concerned—where the "acutely personal" is concerned. Perhaps we think of art as essentially a suppression of the personal in light of genre, of craft, of history. And yet only fifteen years or so after

Eliot's statement, his own admirer published a book that turned such a standard on its head. It did so, moreover, with Eliot's enthusiastic endorsement. The logic of modernism, like that of Emersonian idealism, included autobiography all along. What a poem does when it allows that "personal reminiscence" into the representational plane—more, when it focuses on it, builds a poem around it, allows its inclusion to change the way poems are made—is perhaps the primary subject of this book.

Personae

Starting from Emerson, then, we can see that autobiography is simultaneously an occasion for the imagination and a symptom of its failure, both a highly troped moment and one somehow outside the sphere of literary figuration: however one views it, an issue that still frames our thinking about the function of poetry. The term "autobiography," in fact, is unusually difficult to define. Though repudiations of autobiography abound in modern and postmodern poetry, much of what once counted as "impersonal" now seems like minimally encrypted autobiography. A man named T. S. Eliot tells us, in the person of a man named J. Alfred Prufrock, that while he is "Lazarus, come from the dead" he is by no means "Prince Hamlet, nor was meant to be." Pound introduces himself early as Li-Po's pleading, abandoned river merchant's wife, replying to himself later (in canto 1) in the person of Odysseus, the archetypal itinerant husband. Moore is alternately jerboa and pangolin and, finally, a glacier, an "octopus of ice." In *Harmonium*, Stevens debuts as Peter Quince and, a few pages later, as an indignant bantam rooster. Frost's Witch of Coös, Yeats's Crazy Jane, Crane's Brooklyn Bridge—these are only the most immediately memorable figures among modernism's dramatis personae.

The modernist project that used to be described as "impersonality" was therefore remarkable for its dependence on extreme, even absurd, assumptions of personality. For an art that aimed at "accuracy," or at "the thing itself" or at "economy" (among similar

terms), that sought a poetics undiluted by sensibility, this reflex-
ive assumption of colorful disguise would seem a sign of failure. I
choose the word "assumption" carefully, since I mean to suggest
that these acts of imaginative extension are Whitmanian if not
in scale at least in spirit. "What I assume you shall assume,"
Whitman insists, anticipating, it now seems to us, precisely the
purloined identities we meet in much modernist poetry. But
Whitman's desire to assume what is "commonest, cheapest, nearest and easiest" "to bestow myself on the first that will take me"
is in modernism transformed into a desire to assume the rarest,
dearest, most exotic, and most difficult identities—Stevens's gallery
of burlesques, sometimes embarrassingly Orientalized, Moore's
animals, Frost's gnarled and reticent workmen. The sturdy
American types whom Whitman envisioned are missing from
American modernism, having conceded their place to eccentrics
and curiosities. (William Carlos Williams is perhaps an excep-
tion, but in his work "The pure products of America / Go crazy.")
By this logic, the real experiment that Whitman advertised had
to wait another generation to be carried out, in poems by Sylvia
Plath and Robert Lowell, for example, that found the autobiographical self to be a viable contemporary assumption; and yet
the method of confessionalism depends on locating the self not in
its commonest and nearest forms, among its Whitmanian sturdi-
nesses but, rather, in its rarest and strangest forms, forms fragile
and exotic enough to be, like Moore's pangolins and lizards, a
viable assumption. One way of accounting for the confessional
poetry of Lowell or Plath or Sexton is to say that it courts moments in the formation of the self that are peculiar enough to
reveal themselves in a poetics that had ample means for representing jerboas and pangolins and bantams but comparably few
resources for describing ordinary life.

If "impersonal" modernism could be described as precisely
an analysis of personality, the "sincere" poems that followed it
were often, at their best, analyses of disguise. Early and late in
their careers, we find these poets turning away from naked self-
presentation and toward personae. Indeed when we think of

confessional poetry we now think in terms of the theatricality, Plath's "Lady Lazarus," Sexton's transformations of fairy tale, Berryman's Anne Bradstreet in "Homage to Mistress Bradstreet," Lowell and Bishop in the guises, respectively, of Ulysses and Robinson Crusoe. These uses of personae differed from the strategies of modernism in their desire to find analogies for the autobiographical self, perhaps, rather than photographic negatives. At their best, these autobiographical myths got something said about the uncanny nature of the familiar and near at hand. "Really we had the same life," writes Lowell in his elegy for Berryman, "the generic one our generation offered." The horror of living a merely paradigmatic, never fully individualized, life is a particularly rich subject for lyric poetry, with its own ongoing adjustments between self and paradigm, voice and form. "I am green with envy at your kind of assurance," wrote Bishop on the eve of the publication of *Life Studies*, "all you have to do is put down the names, and the sense that it seems significant, American, etc. gives you the confidence to tackle any theme, no matter how difficult" (*One Art*, 351). And yet in a mature poetics like Lowell's, one's own name is not really put down but put on, and done so as a linguistically dense act, an act of troping. What makes Lowell's poetry so interesting today is the feeling that his own name constitutes the most onerous of assumptions, not only for its historical association with the genocidal New England aristocracy but also for its tendency to represent the dynamic processes of unfolding life in static, unchanging terms.

But what if these categories of candor and reticence are finally a cul-de-sac? After all, the sensation of personhood is as vivid when one withholds as when one confides; both acts, withholding and confiding, happen at extraordinarily close range, in an acoustics of the personal and individualized. The compound act of assuming the name Henry, as John Berryman did for the duration of his *Dream Songs*, and then making this Henry identical to himself, the historical John Berryman, in every pungent detail, could happen only within a poetic culture where the self makes an enormously galvanized claim on our attention. The dimensions of this claim are clearest when seen in terms of the tenets of the Language school, whose reprimand to mainstream lyric poetry is the sternest and most intellectually vigorous in recent years. Many poets and critics who had presumed to be operating, in both their semiotic and their practical politics, on the frontiers of the left were alarmed to receive missives from the previously unimaginably leftist territory called Language poetry. What those missives said was that referentiality itself was ideology and that the endless deferrals and deflections of referentiality enacted by the lyric, the "ambiguities" that William Empson described, were only mystifications of its power. Furthermore the self, no matter how deeply or searchingly interrogated, was a guileful deception. Here is Charles Bernstein: "It's a mistake to posit the self as the primary organizing feature of writing. As many others have pointed out, a poem exists in a matrix of social and historical relations that are more significant to the formation of an individual text than any personal qualities of the life or voice of an author" (Perloff, *Dance* 219). It's an idea that one is inclined to agree with, but it has been notoriously difficult to implement in poetic praxis. Language poetry obliterated certain kinds of poems that would have quietly evaporated anyway, namely, the "voice"-centered workshop poem and the late-confessional poem of ritualized masculinity; but in practice, since it has indulged itself in a poetry of interchangeable filigreed surfaces, it has failed to give us works that delight and instruct—even in its own austere senses of those terms. Like all poems of filigreed surface—Hopkins and Crane come to mind— Language poems detain us for an inordinate amount of time at the level of signifier, but in Language poetry we aren't assigned enough work there to occupy us, and in any case we're forbidden, by the logic of the mode, from doing the kind of work we want to do, namely, matching signifier to referent. Nevertheless, from the vantage point of the Language school we can see that the assumption of self, whether one's own or another's, is always a theoretically inflected act, and today operates against a ready and fully articulated critique.

One Kind of Everything

I now wish to turn to the question of what claim, if any, "auto-biographical" poets have to being "representative" of selves other than their own. What vision of the common do we find in po-ets like Bishop (whose perceptions are importantly singular) or O'Hara (whose "many-footed Manhattan" is a small world of orbiting coteries)?

Whitmanian catalog is almost always an affair of types. Part of what allows Whitman the rapid shuffling of attention that catalog demands is his ability to make split-second taxonomical decisions: butcher boy, contralto, suicide, gander, moose. Often Whitman seems to have known enough examples of a given type even to predict "offstage" outcomes or narratives he would never be able to confirm. (He knows, for example, that the "lunatic" being conveyed to the asylum once slept in a "cot by his mother's bed.") This kind of remark is central to Whitman, who lives on an island, "million-footed Manhattan," where individuals blur into the aggregate mass of human enterprise. When Elizabeth Bishop writes (in the voice of Crusoe, in "Crusoe in England") that *her* island has merely "one kind of everything," I believe she means to revise the specifically Whitmanian poetics of catalog. It is the problem of selves hyperspecified (the way Robinson Crusoe was and the way Walt Whitman often was not) to have no means of extrapolating from their selves (island like, "isolated") to com-monly and socially held reality.

If Bishop and others find Whitmanian catalog impossible, given the hyperspecificity and isolation of American subjectiv-ity since Whitman, nevertheless the terms of engagement are, for poets of Bishop's generation and later, still explicitly Whit-manian. The difficulty of knowing communities, relationships, nations—the world outside the self—if a person feels truly that there is "one kind of everything"—this is a Whitmanian problem (or at the very least, a problem Whitman caused). I chose Bishop's phrase for this book's title because I feel it crystallizes this prob-lem, so central to our poets, of writing the autobiographical self in a culture where claims based on such a self are treated (rightly, I think) with scrutiny.

There are other good reasons for thinking of contemporary American poets as especially indebted to Whitman. The desire to describe selves as ongoing creative acts, reiterative acts of becoming, is especially marked in Whitman, who writes often in a kind of future-perfect tense that allows him to see what his words will have been, how and by whom he will have been read. For this reason the self in Whitman is not just "cellular" as Philip Fisher has argued in *Still the New World*, made up of small subunits like a crowd whose organic whole is made up of individual hurrying men and women, but also episodic, happening in time as an unfolding event. In Whitman, terms like "self" and "nation" (and "crowd") are not essentially infinitely accretive but rather infinitely divisible. A new experience in the self's formation, a death or a marriage, does not add to a pile of experiences whose height could be infinite; rather, it takes its place within an existing body, the way dividing cells take their place within, even as they renew, the existing body. By this logic all subsequent acts of self-formation take their place within an existing, infinitely divisible, body. My claim is that each of the five poets I discuss here "happen," as an event, within the already-complete Whitmanian body. It is not so simple a thing as pointing to O'Hara's prosodic effervescence, Bidart's Whitmanian erotics, Lowell's oracular stance, et cetera: stylistic affinities are interesting but only take us so far into the larger question of how American poetry of the private, exquisitely individuated self can be seen as sufficiently all-encompassing to answer the Whitmanian call.

In "Crossing Brooklyn Ferry," Whitman describes the open, infinitely divisible body of "the crowd":

> Crowds of men and women attired in the usual costumes, how
>   curious you are to me!
> On the ferry-boats the hundreds and hundreds that cross,
>   returning home, are more curious to me than you suppose,

And you that shall cross from shore to shore years hence are more to
me, and more in my meditations, than you might suppose.

(*Leaves* 159)

The crowd is defined by its uniformity, its "usual costumes"
and unfluctuating movement, every day, twice a day, at the ap-
pointed hours. This crowd is not, as in the London scenes of
Wordsworth's *Prelude*, an aggregate or composite whose individual aspects remain, though fragmented, visible. There, individual affect and gesture become grotesquely memorable, as we
see men's faces seeming to bob atop a current, little poignant
or violent vignettes splintered off from their narrative contexts,
what Wordsworth calls "the perpetual whirl / Of trivial objects."
In "Crossing Brooklyn Ferry" the crowd is rather a kind of average, where every new member of the crowd is attired in the "usual
costume," namely, the costume of the crowd. The crowd exists,
permanently, and as the hundredth member joins the crowd he
is incorporated into its body. The idea of "usual" behavior or
events implies that at any point in the stream of time we can
dip in our toe and the water will be the same temperature, the
current the same strength. This profound stability of shape over
time allows Whitman to describe even the movements of future
men and women, even our own movements, since we exist within
one temporal body.

Whitman bequeaths to later American poets a way of being,
while stylistically distinct, nevertheless part of the assembled
crowd of citizen-readers. When in the above passage the "you"
changes, from the first instance when the addressee is "crowds"
to the second where the addressee, separate from the crowds, is
asked to observe the crowds, to the third where the addressee
is part of a new crowd, assembled through time, Whitman is
undertaking an experiment in poetic temporality. He is asking,
in essence, not for agreement but for fulfillment—in crossing
from one shore (his own actual, historical shore in Brooklyn in
the mid-nineteenth century) to another (ours, one hundred-odd

years later), he asks us to view the specificities of historical change as accidental or illusory, in light of the manifest continuities of human life. The crowd that assembles on a ferryboat on a single day in Brooklyn in 1870 becomes the crowd that gathers, one by one, to read "Crossing Brooklyn Ferry" through time. This crowd averages individual styles and claims, but only because it admits such a diversity of styles and claims. When later American poets "tell us how it is with them" to use Emerson's phrase from "The Poet" they do so as part of a Whitmanian chorus of poet-citizens—no matter how ingrown, gnarled, or eccentric the testimony they deliver may be.

Though the crowd we join is "abstract" (to use Fisher's term) from Whitman's point of view, an average of all the available types, already complete though infinitely divisible, Whitman is from our point of view vivid and distinct—enough so to be a "character." What he assumes we assume, especially when we assume his own identity, as later American poets often have. He instructs us how to assume the identity of "Walt Whitman," perhaps, by treating identity as always already an assumption. In David Reynolds's account, the "real" Whitman was "to a large degree an actor": "He developed a theatrical style in his daily behavior. When he grew his beard and adopted his distinctive casual dress in the fifties, people on the street, intrigued by his unusual appearance, tried to guess who he might be. Was he a sea captain? A smuggler? A clergyman? A slave trader? One of his friends, William Roscoe Thayer, called him a 'poseur of truly colossal proportions, one to whom playing a part had long before become so habitual that he ceased to be conscious he was doing it'" (Reynolds 161). One striking fact about American poetry in the wake of Whitman is how often the poet is invoked by name, in poems from Wallace Stevens's "Like Decorations in a Nigger Cemetery" to Allen Ginsberg's "A Supermarket in California" to Lowell's late poem "Shadow," which begins:

> I must borrow from Walt Whitman to praise this night,
> twice waking me smiling, mysteriously in full health,

twice delicately calling me to the world.
Praise be to sleep and sleep's one god,
the Voyeur, the Mother,
Job's tempestuous, inconstant I AM . . .
who soothes the doubtful murmurs of the heart.
(Lowell, Collected Poems 826)

In Frank Bidart's account of these lines, the "borrowing" is from
Whitman's poem "The Sleepers," where sleep is described as a
balm for the sick, where *"the swell'd and convuls'd and congested
awake to themselves in condition"* (Lowell, *Collected Poems* 1147).
As though Whitman provided, through his own porous identity,
a portal into still other identities, we move through him immediately to "Job's tempestuous, inconstant I AM." This layered,
palimpsest-like statement could of course be said by anybody,
which is why it is both a "borrowing" and a viable assertion of
identity. It is paradoxical to attribute the proof of one's existence to a preexisting textual assertion. But when Whitman is
here conjured, we sense to what a great degree the Whitmanian
stance was already, for Whitman, a performance, though one
that is almost intuitive to the American understanding of self.
Here, on the very edge of sleep, when the socialized self (and
with it the learning necessary to know oneself from Whitman or
from Job, or to know Whitman from Job) would be utterly inca-
pacitated, Lowell finds not himself but a "borrowing." Whether
he finally is Whitman, who tames "sleep's one god" with his
honeyed prayer, or Job ravaged by the tempests of a God's wrath,
or Robert Lowell, writing in the mid-1970's, becomes an open
question.

The breadth of the Whitmanian conception of self, its essentially compound or "cellular" nature, poses a challenge for later
writers who would speak more narrowly of their own experiences. The skepticism of a Charles Bernstein is, I would guess,
Whitmanian in spirit—at least insofar as it denies anyone, no
matter how immense her claim, the right to self-representation.
The ambitious poetries of modernism and postmodernism have

all displayed a strongly antisubjective strain, whether we think in terms of George Oppen's minimalist gizmos or Pound's opposing conception of poetry as simultaneously annals, a textbook, and a stone column—anything, that is, but a personal testimony. It is a strange turn of events that subjective life would become dismissible as material for lyric poetry, when at least since the Romantics there was an available theoretical argument on its behalf. Schiller's distinction between "naive" and "sentimental" poetry is here pertinent, since it represents a failed wager on what modernism would eventually be like. Schiller believed that it was precisely "interestedness" that distinguished the modern, "sentimental" man. M. H. Abrams writes: "Modern, or 'sentimental' man, no longer in unity with nature or himself . . . tends in poetry to substitute his ideal for the given reality, and also 'can suffer no impression without immediately attending to his own part in the performance'" (238).

Schillerian "sentimentality" did not in fact come to define the modern, at least insofar as the modern is synonymous with modernism. Rather, a series of checks on sentiment, many of them premised on scientific discourse, became the rule. The result was a new kind of "objectivity," mirroring the existing structures, some of them astonishingly intricate, of reality. When Moore seeks out her creatures she does so because her appetite for intricacy of design, and for the moral qualities of forbearance and cleverness it suggests, is not satisfied by human behavior; but her preference for the intricacies of mollusks over the intricacies of men must be understood as a means of bringing the intricacies of men into relief. This strategy, like Eliot's "objective correlative," suggests that to some degree subjective life must be coaxed, rather than summoned, into view, that it will not answer when called by its own name. This suspicion of subjectivity as a means becomes, for many writers, a suspicion of subjectivity even as an end, even as an idea. Susan Stewart quotes Theodor Adorno's description of lyric poetry's ability to "turn subjectivity into objectivity": "The highest lyric works are those in which the subject, with no remaining trace of mere matter, sounds forth in language until language itself acquires a voice. . . . This is why the lyric reveals itself to be the most deeply grounded in society when it does not chime in with society, when it communicates nothing" (Stewart, *Poetry* 44). Adorno would argue, I think, that the cultural silence of lyric performs cultural work, establishing a use for language that resists easy commodification; but that means not that lyric poetry ought to court a deliberate frivolity or nihilism in order to be incommunicative but, rather, that the capacity of lyric-become-silent vis-à-vis culture is most striking when it seems most unlikely, as when lyric seems manifestly to be embracing culture.

The poets I discuss here become themselves by becoming Whitman, but become Whitman, equally, by becoming themselves. Louise Glück's passionate investigation into the authority of lyric speakers results in her detaching speech from its immediate social contexts, so that it attains the strangeness and impersonality of song. She has written poems meant to be heard as arias, as hymns, as pop songs—even (in *Meadowlands*) a sequence of duets for the two halves, eerily alike, that result when the compound self of a marriage splits. Hers is a Whitmanian project in that it sees the self as "many selves" and in doing so asks what kind of self a lyric poem constitutes. It is Whitmanian as well for its interest in the identities of crowds, albeit the smaller crowds that cluster around a display of flowers or a grocery case full of cheeses. We see this phenomenon is Glück's "Formaggio":

> Tributaries
> feeding into a large river: I had
> many lives. In the provisional world,
> I stood where the fruit was,
> flats of cherries, clementines,
> under Hallie's flowers.
>
> I had many lives. Feeding
> into a river, the river
> feeding into a great ocean. If the self
> becomes invisible has it disappeared?

> I thrived. I lived
> not completely alone, alone
> but not completely, strangers
> surging around me.
>   (*Vita Nova* 13)

In her description of the loss and reclamation of selfhood within the crowd, "strangers surging around me," Glück is allegorizing the perpetual ebb and flow of self within language—which is why the poem and the cheese shop it describes share a name, and why the proper names of the quotidian are preserved here for display. We lose ourselves, Glück suggests, in the absorptive experiences of daily life, only to find ourselves later, perhaps in the composition of a poem, "whole." But in composing the poem we again disappear into the communal, into the "crowd" of words that (like Whitman's crowd of commuters from shore to shore) simultaneously precede and succeed us.

In this sense of the self as constituted by its immediacies, place names and proper names like "Formaggio" and "Fishmonger" replace the name "Louise Glück." This sense—that the arbitrarily placed but inarguably "there" world of shops and shopkeepers, for its stability over time, its uncanny steadiness in relation to one's own "comings and goings," is better mooring than one's own private world—is in part derived from Frank O'Hara. O'Hara's Whitmanian inheritance is easier to identify than Glück's, situated as it is in Whitman's own "million-footed Manhattan" and sharing Whitman's poetics of rapidity and flux. O'Hara's "I-do-this-I-do-that" poems are a kind of literalized catalog, in which walking down a city street replaces the rhetorical instancing, without syntactic hierarchy, of the catalog. Like Glück, O'Hara thinks of the self as permeable by the world of fact, though the sheer volume of facts recorded by that self, and the poem that embodies it, would indicate that no one fact takes root in consciousness. Indeed many of O'Hara's poems (such as "The Day Lady Died," which I discuss at length later in this volume) read like accounts of how his own method fails—how his desire to locate the poem solely in the adjacencies of ordinary life is thwarted by memory. The nubbiness, the insoluble proximity, of ordinary life is paradoxically obliterated by experiences that are evaporative and distant, like the memory, through the haze of smoke and intoxication, of Billie Holiday's voice.

The loss and reclamation of the self within the crowd is not only a Whitmanian figure, then, but an enactment of Whitmanian inheritance—since the "crowd" is one that assembles around the spectacle of a great poet articulating a poetic project with national significance. There are, of course, other figures for the loss of self and its eventual recovery in contemporary American poetry. Frank Bidart's sequence "The Hours of the Night" is an account of how in darkness the self disappears, like even the nearest and most familiar accoutrements it has arranged around itself. Each of these "Hours" (there have been three thus far) seems to carry us as far from the immediate world as conceivable into a preexisting world of artifact that we find, much against our expectation, includes us. Bidart's erotic entering and reentering of the Ovidian story of Cinyras and Myrrha (which I treat in the chapter on Bidart) mirrors the daughter's transgressive entering and reentering of her father's bedroom; her seduction of him suggests Bidart's own coaxing of a poetic "father" to his ends, his ends being the completion of the poem, the living through another "Hour" of the night. The flight into permanence, in this case not so much the permanence of "myth" as the permanence of text, is never itself permanent; just as we can't live forever on our lunch hours, as O'Hara might want, and can't keep a cot at the cheese shop, as Glück might wish, we can't sustain ourselves in Ovid. The text has a beginning, a middle, and an end, and at its end we are forced to put the book down. Bidart's "Hours" end with the ritual valediction, "this is the end of the [*X*] hour of the night," like the chiming of a bell. The statement constitutes the (textually bound) recovery of the self that exists outside of the text.

When Bishop constructs a Whitmanian fable about identity, its dissolution within the common and its subsequent, always temporary reformation as poetic performance, she finds the first occasion in her career to call herself by her own first name. "In the Waiting Room" is a recollection of accompanying an adult, Bishop's fictional "Aunt Consuelo," to "keep her dentist's appointment." It is as though adulthood itself were an appointment one could not but keep, with childhood its waiting room. The poem includes the following scene of self-recognition, a damaged syllogism at its heart:

> I said to myself: three days
> and you'll be seven years old.
> I was saying it to stop
> the sensation of falling off
> the round, turning world
> into cold, blue-black space.
> But I felt: you are an *I*,
> you are an *Elizabeth*,
> you are one of *them*.
>   (*Poems* 183)

The formulation "You are an I" is easily inverted, of course, so that the sensation of selfhood for Bishop often seems closer to its inversion "I am a you." (It is this sensation of being a specified other that I explore in my pages on her.) As we pass from anonymous singularity (the sensation of being an "I") to anonymous plurality (the sensation of being "one of them"), we do so, Bishop suggests, through our own name, which "identifies" us in the crudest sense but which carries no information whatsoever about our authenticated identities. The question of one's being "an Elizabeth" (or a Frank, or a Robert, or a Louise) versus *being Elizabeth* (Bishop does not say "You are *Elizabeth*") refers to this anonymous or averaged spot in identity, precisely in the place where one expected to find a definitely specified core of identity. When John Ashbery calls poetic language a "visible core" he is pointing out that where language is concerned our ordinary bias against surface—our sense that surface is a mask or armor for depth, that our rarest and most meaningful possessions are hidden—need not apply. The nearest Bishop can come to identity is by saying something to herself, in this case her age, comically accurate down to the day, and by feeling something, in this case the mingled horror and pleasure of being identified. The next thing we learn about Bishop is that she has a point of view, a radicalized optics that allows her to see only knees, hands, boots—bodies as fragmented as the bodies transformed by Spleen in Pope's "Rape of the Lock" or the bodies swallowed whole by the crowd in the lines from Wordsworth mentioned above. Bishop gives a "sidelong glance":

> I scarcely dared to look
> to see what it was I was.
> I gave a sidelong glance
> —I couldn't look any higher—
> at shadowy gray knees,
> trousers and skirts and boots
> and different pairs of hands
> lying under the lamps.
>
> (*Poems* 183)

This fragmented blazon of adulthood, terrifying given one's own perceptual restrictions, is what one "sees" from the point of view of steadied, fixed identity. Throughout her poems what Bishop argues is that it is our perceptions that differentiate us, which speak most accurately of where and among whom we sit "In the Waiting Room." The mingled terror and wonder that Bishop feels in this poem (in regard to these dental patients but also in regard to a "naked, black woman" in the pages of a *National Geographic* she reads to pass the time) arises from "seeing what it was I was"—from finding evidence of one's own identity strewn about the world outside the self. "What it was I was" is, by the way, perhaps the most accurate, most mordantly beautiful, epitaph imaginable.

The experience of losing oneself in the crowd is always, I would suggest, a way of describing the losses of self within language that poetry both enacts and describes. This connection between crowds and words is one Whitman makes explicit, in his assertion that we readers of "Crossing Brooklyn Ferry" constitute a crowd, assembled through time, analogous to the crowd of commuters assembled on a ferryboat. Whether we lose ourselves in linguistic data (as in O'Hara) or in our own first name (as in Bishop), lyric poetry becomes a site where experiences of loss and recovery of identity can be not merely described but also enacted. This is perhaps especially true for the many poets of our "autobiographical" age who turn to personae in rendering themselves. Only O'Hara among the poets I discuss here lacks this interest in personae as a kind of gauze curtain through which identity is glimpsed or, when the wind gusts, suddenly faced. Bishop's early personae, like Lowell's, were obscure, but the two poets turn late in their careers to the use of canonically central myths, myths commonly held, even memorized and called up from memory. For Lowell, autobiography could not but become myth, since his own identity had (for him) long ago coagulated into heirlooms and lore. "Ulysses and Circe" is one of the great autobiographical poems in our literature but it records not a single fact about Lowell's life. It makes no disclosures of any kind. By the time it was written, Lowell, like the figure of Odysseus, existed in many conflicting versions; only a figure so mercurial, so enticing to acts of reinterpretation could represent the self as it is constituted over a long life of writing one's life. Odysseus exists in the cultural imagination exactly as the self exists in the individual imagination, Lowell suggests—as a palimpsest of inscriptions and reinscriptions. This is why Lowell chooses the Latin form of Odysseus's name, and why the poem begins with a rendering of Dante's Ulysses Canto rather than with a passage from Homer. Bishop likewise turns to a version of the Robinson Crusoe story blurred by reiteration, abstracted by its long residence in her memory. In "Crusoe in England," autobiographically consequential feelings like loneliness and nostalgia find articulation in a story, Crusoe's, which stands in for Bishop's own. Only the rough outline of the Crusoe story is relevant here, in a poem that fulfills itself by means of the same exquisite perceptual detail and tone as Bishop's other, more directly autobiographical poems. At certain important moments in the poem, Crusoe seems to have access to Bishop's own memory and to the shared cultural memory of which he is himself a canonical constituent. The picture of the self that emerges is a complex aggregate of personal, literary, perceptual, and cultural events—a crowded self, itself a crowd.

Reading Objects: Robert Lowell

The work of Robert Lowell is marked by its pronounced use of autobiographical facts and by a profound, counterpointed skepticism about the poetic use of such facts. His career reads like an alternating conjuring, and subsequent repudiation, of the personal life. Lowell's temperament from the start was antipersonal, occasionally to an absurd extent: he is said to have written, during his freshman year at Harvard, an epic on the First Crusade. His early poems are apocalyptic renderings of local sites and tend toward dire and overheated prophecy. Lowell's early style came to seem to him rigid and shrill, a "goliath's armor of brazen metric," as he says of Milton. Lowell himself came to see those early poems as a displacement onto history of his own hysteria and turned, in the late fifties, to writing the muted and personal poems that would make up his book *Life Studies*. *Life Studies* and the poems it inspired—poems of the so-called confessional school—depict the shocks of family life in the American milieu, doing so in a more-or-less conversational idiom, an idiom meant to surprise by its informality, and employing a Freudian logic of repression and recovery. Lowell's first nakedly "factual" poems date from this period, where Lowell seems to want to transform as little as possible to realia while still making them available to representation.

Lowell's use of autobiographical facts sparked an immediate scandal; among his contemporaries it was felt that excessive factuality violated the decorum of lyric poetry, a standard that modernism, with its emphasis on poetic impersonality, had reinforced. Lowell's work seemed, compared with the poems of his immediate predecessors and indeed with his own early poems, "sensational." (There was a countervailing enthusiasm for the book, of course, on the part of readers who liked sensationalism.) Later in Lowell's career, his critics' indictment of his excessive facticity seems to have been partly internalized—indeed his sublimely remorseful last poem, "Epilogue," states the case against facticity most eloquently:

> Those blessed structures, plot and rhyme,
> why are they no help to me now
> I want to make
> something imagined, not recalled?
> (*Collected Poems*)

The poem stages a problem—"my poetry doesn't adequately satisfy my desire 'to make' anymore, so anchored is it in the brute 'facts' of life"—which it won't fully resolve, so at the end of Lowell's career we are left with an indictment so severely persuasive that it seems irrefutable. You build an edifice, and then you tear it down—this was the formula for Yeats and Stevens, two of Lowell's masters. But somehow in those earlier poets the tearing down seemed more vigorous, more a flexing of imaginative muscle. "[The] absence of imagination / had itself to be imagined," writes Stevens (502), whose refusal to write down his own first-order experiences was sustained to the very end. Lowell's remorseful formula substitutes the "recalled" for the "imagined"—consigning poetry to the mere recording of "what happened."

Lowell's self-critique is primarily an aesthetic one, a matter of taste, and as such it conjures its own refutation. "I like my poetry *recalled*," someone might say—"I think that the imagination is overrated." ("I have always been / more interested in truth than in imagination" [James Schuyler, "A Few Days"]). But poetic style isn't merely an aesthetic matter, of course (by which I mean, aesthetics isn't merely an aesthetic matter). In the years since Lowell's death, a more substantial critique of Lowell's work has taken hold. This critique supposes that Lowell's autobiographical facticity reflects a narrow—and a now politically and philosophically discredited—model of the self. This newer critique is complex and far-reaching enough to merit a long study all its own, since it mirrors a general turn in the culture of poetry, what Stephen Burt has called the "epistemological turn." Poets don't conceive of "selves" as concatenations of facts, anymore, the argument goes, but rather epistemological or perceptual processes. Poets like A. R. Ammons or Jorie Graham explore the relation between cognition and its objects or between the body and the sense data that bombards it. The world's resistance to cognitive mastery is often figured, in poets like Ammons and Graham, as a superabundance, a turmoil too wild to be tamed: Stevens's "The Auroras of Autumn," with its serpentine and annihilating sky, is the ancestor of this kind of contemporary poem. For Ammons and Graham, in the time it takes to name existing phenomena, new phenomena are always taking shape; the mind is therefore always lagging behind experience.

This so-called epistemological turn is related, also, to a linguistic turn, exemplified by poets of the Language school. The tendency of language toward unruliness, and the subsequent institutional need to affix meaning to otherwise errant, subversive signifiers, provides Language poets with their theoretical frame. Language poets have located the crisis point for lyric, then, in the corruptions of denotative language itself and have written intentionally unreadable poems to resist those corruptions. Both Language poets and "epistemological" poets employ factual data, in Ammons's case to show the limits of cognitive mastery, in the Language poets' case to show the fallibility of denotative language; but significant autobiographical fact, the sort of fact Lowell so often employs, is anathema to these poets for whom the notion of linguistic determinacy is itself naive.

The suspicion of facticity dovetails with larger, more naggingly ad hominem, suspicions of Lowell. His friend Elizabeth Bishop expressed this rather brutal point cordially, in a famous letter to Lowell: "I must confess . . . that I am green with envy of your kind of assurance. I feel that I could write in as much detail about my uncle Artie, say—but what would be the significance? Nothing at all. . . . Whereas all you have to do is put down the names! And the fact that it seems significant, illustrative, American, etc., gives you, I think, the confidence you display about tackling any idea or theme, seriously, in both writing and conversation" (*One Art* 351). Lowell's "assurance" comes from the steadying effect of his impeccable "Americanness," which provides, for his otherwise uneventful details, an "illustrative" quality, a quality of speaking beyond the confines of any one self. This very assurance has come to seem more and more like appropriation, though, as the meaning of the signifier "American" has itself shifted and slipped, growing ever more indeterminate as the signified, the American citizenry, has evolved. Mark Strand, writing in the 1990s, expresses the going view of Lowell's "assurance": "Lowell would like to bury his past, but needs it for the mythologizing of himself. As a consequence, the mythic portentousness of some of his poems is full of self-mocking irony. . . . The confessional poet's need to document his life with facts gives his poetry a chatty quality. . . . His insecurity and consequent mania for naming keep him from being a truly subjective poet. He names in order to possess, and possessing, in turn, is part of what helps him to account for himself" (Strand 112). For Strand and for many others, the heart of the problem seems to be Lowell's "need to document his life with facts," an urge Strand connects with the desire to "possess." In this account Lowell becomes a little like the "hermit heiress" in his poem "Skunk Hour" who "buys up all the eyesores facing her shore / and lets them fall." Lowell's acquisitiveness is of course a condition of immense privilege, since (to extend the conceit) only the very rich can make possession the minimal requirement of selfhood. Lowell seemingly keeps even our attention by these means, buying it with the inflated capital of his significant facts. Strand thinks Lowell's need for external corroboration, his taste for bric-a-brac "keeps him from being a truly subjective poet," meaning a poet alert to the subtleties of consciousness as it weighs and assesses the perceptual world. A reader even superficially acquainted with Strand's own work will know immediately what at least one "truly subjective" poetry might sound like—namely, like Strand's own poetry, with its sly way of seeing realia at a slant.

Robert Lowell cannot be read satisfyingly without an interest, on his reader's part, in autobiography—an interest, that is, in the way the self is constituted in the social world, by means of autobiographical fact: the names and dates that plot us on the various grids that constitute familial, social, and political life. (If you think that such data have no place in lyric poetry, you won't enjoy reading Lowell.) These are as much a fundamental part of his subjectivity as Strand's still lifes and impressionistic seascapes. It is probably too late in reading culture to dismiss poets entirely for their subject matter; we no longer have taboo subjects, only more or less easily retrievable ones. Lowell chose one of the least retrievable, most dismissible ones: his own family. He deserves credit for his boldness alone. But Lowell's primary interest isn't in autobiography per se but, rather, in two problems related to auto-biography. The first is, how might autobiographical fact—which normally has meaning only in social discourse—be successfully integrated back into imaginative and emotional life and the forms of art that proceed from them? The second, nearly inverse prob-lem, is how might the private self—the self most intelligible in lyric poetry—be integrated into the social and, particularly, the political world? "I'm tired. Everyone's tired of my turmoil," Low-ell laments at the end of "Eye and Tooth." That "everyone" means not only Lowell's intimate circle but, allegorically, the "everyone" that constitutes the nation. How might poets, "turmoil"-ridden necessarily, also be citizens? How might citizens, as citizens, also be poets?

Lowell's critics have long worried about the problem of how such an inveterately private poet could claim for himself a public role. I will not seek an answer to that question here but, rather, show how Lowell makes poems out of posing that question to himself. I am especially interested here in how Lowell makes autobiography (to quote Stevens) "a little hard to see"—often literally hard to see: as I will show, Lowell's frequent tropes of compromised sight—boarded windows, scratched corneas, lost glasses—are ways of talking about his own vexed desire to extend himself into the common world and (conversely) to integrate the common world into the imagination. Lowell is always "reading" his autobiography and, often (as I will show), is literally reading it, inscribed on book jackets, in his own earlier poems, on tombstones and memorial statues. His "significance" is not a fixed or settled fact but a fact that requires constant, vigorous recognition.

Three Reading Acts: "Father's Bedroom," "Blizzard in Cambridge," and "For the Union Dead"

"Emotion" in Lowell, writes Alan Williamson, is often "held at a distance by . . . the relentless, documentary accumulation of facts: place names, brand-names, dates, bits of history, and objects, objects, objects, each one handled with the meticulousness of an Agassiz" (Williamson, *Monsters* 55). Williamson is regarding an aspect of Lowell that depends on what might be called a modernist evasion of subjectivity by means of what Marianne Moore names (in "An Octopus") "relentless accuracy" and defines as "capacity for fact." The cultural mood that could prompt Yvor Winters, tired of poetic license, to call for a "Poet's Handbook to Science" is often Lowell's mood; and yet Lowell's facts are not scientific but historical and (as a subset of the historical) personal. His poems are filled with "bric-a-brac": old photographs, odd volumes of old books, beer cans, oil portraits, and at least one pair of gigantic upholstered dice are the details that spring immediately to mind. These facts and factlike objects bear themselves differently from Moore's or Pound's facts, asking precisely how much emotion might be shown to inhere in mere things.

I want now to consider a poem that would seem easily dismissible, based on the various cases against Lowell I have sketched above. "Father's Bedroom" is a poem that even those sympathetic to Lowell describe as "interesting only if one is already interested in Lowell" (Sontag and Graham 17). It is a simple, nearly a slight, poem, but it provides an arresting example of what mere facts can convey in Lowell's hands. The poem's only ambition is, it seems, to inventory the contents of Lowell's father's bedroom after his death. Such a poem would only be possible, of course, in the larger context of elegiac recollection and recovery *Life Studies* provides, but that context, pungently rendered elsewhere in the book, is here kept offstage. The poem opens with a low-key inventory:

> In my Father's bedroom:
> blue threads as thin
> as pen-writing on the bedspread,
> blue dots on the curtains,
> a blue kimono,
> Chinese sandals with blue plush straps.
> (*Collected Poems* 177)

When we read a catalog like this one, we think immediately of Whitman. Indeed one could say about this poem that it shows how much American poetry had conceded in one hundred years. Whitman's lists seek, by judicious selection of exempla, to traverse otherwise untraversable territories: bringing together, and so calling into consciousness, phenomena ordinarily too widely dispersed to be seen as cognate. The act of yoking together such widely dispersed exempla contributes to Whitman's effect of extravagance, the sense of a consciousness neither borne on nor bound by one set of eyes and ears. Whitman can see inside the bedrooms and kitchens of anyone he pleases, gymnastically leaping from site to site, reporting their contents with great precision and gusto. The very notion of catalog, with its expansiveness, its minimal subordination and syntax, implies abundance, volume, both a world of fact too various to be conceptualized and a concept too evasive to be immediately evident. But Lowell's sad list implies just the opposite, as though the whole world amounted to only these few nearby objects, each one itself worn "from hard usage." Lowell, withdrawing his imagination from every corner of the earth but one, finds even that one to be devoid of the remarkable. It is as though the poem itself were lit not by the lamp of poetic inspiration but by the doily-shaded bed lamp it describes.

But "Father's Bedroom" is as philosophically ambitious as any poem in Lowell, precisely because it narrows its vision so radically. The details of Lowell's father's bedroom would be evident, presumably, to anyone, so that the act of reading comes to seem like a means of providing corroboration, as though Lowell has said "come over here and see something." In limiting himself to what anyone might observe, Lowell consigns everyone to his observations; there is nothing arguable in the scene, no leap of association, no insight that could plausibly provoke resistance or skepticism. Poems that depend on visual detail (Bishop's poem "The Fish" comes to mind) tend toward descriptive ingenuity, as though poetry had a different, a deeper, set of eyes than ours. When Bishop describes the eyeball of "The Fish" as being "packed / with tarnished tinfoil / seen through the lenses / of old scratched isinglass" we sense the radical singularity, the ingenuity, of her perceptual powers, an ingenuity demanded and inspired by the wild, surprising beauty of a fish's eyeball. We can endorse such a description—indeed we do so, immediately and happily—but to call it "true" or "false," "accurate" or "inaccurate" would be beside the point. In Lowell's poem, however, description is given an absurdly narrow set of parameters within which to work: metaphorical figuration is almost entirely absent and, where present ("blue threads as thin / as pen-writing on the bedspread"), it seems off-hand, almost perfunctory, only a step or two removed from literal description. The poem's self-imposed stylistic gauntness is most striking in the repetition, against all possible aesthetic counsel, of the word "blue." If poetry has any obligations whatsoever, one wants to say, mustn't they include the duty to spot the differences above or below the common "blueness" of four blue things? And yet if there were a fifth blue thing in the "Father's Bedroom," it would also be called "blue" and so on and so on, ad infinitum. To name each blue thing in the room separately, calling each of them by the same bland name, seems virtually to abandon entirely poetry's powers of imaginative discernment.

But the repetition of the word "blue" establishes the poem's stark representational contract, a contract stipulating that things be "coldly noted" (in Allen Tate's phrase), retaining their common names, perhaps the names that Lowell's father himself might have assigned them. The trouble with this technique is that such names are usually insufficiently meaning-bearing to constitute, all by themselves, a lyric poem. However one defines the necessary and sufficient conditions of lyric, "Father's Bedroom" would seem not to satisfy them. But the act of withdrawing one's imaginative resources from an object is itself a meaningful act, an act of the imagination—and, where the object is a highly significant site like the one Lowell describes, an act of great emotional force. The poem's imaginative starkness, furthermore, allows the surfaces of its constituent objects to speak for themselves, which they do with surprising poignancy. To begin with, nearly every object described possesses a filigreed or adorned surface, a layer of sense data manifestly above its ordinarily outermost surface: the "bedspread" wrapping the bed is itself wrapped in "pen-like" threads, the curtains are covered with "blue dots," the lamp is covered by a "doily-shade," the floor is "sandpapered":

> The broad-planked floor
> had a sandpapered neatness.
> The clear glass bed-lamp
> with a white doily shade
> was still raised a few

inches by resting on volume two
of Lafcadio Hearn's
Glimpses of Unfamiliar Japan.
      (*Collected Poems* 177)

Each of these details is a kind of overlay, somewhat like a written text, which is complex enough, sufficiently involved with human wishes, to be meaningful. The significant content of things, in this poem, is whatever is nearest to us and most immediately evident, not, as is often the case in poems, what is hidden or obscure. The poem, lacking our imaginative extension into its terrain, seems, by presenting a series of ever-nearer surfaces, to extend itself into ours. But since each new detail seems to require, and to imply, closer inspection than the last, together they chart a tiny progress through the bedroom as we move from perceptual to physical and finally to emotional involvement. The blueness of bedspreads and polka dots is legible from several feet away, perhaps from the threshold of the room; but in order to feel the "sandpapered smoothness" of floors we have to be walking on them, and in order to see that the "glass bed-lamp" rests on Lafcadio Hearn's *Glimpses of Unfamiliar Japan* and not another book, and on "volume two" instead of volume one, we must have surrendered the consolations of distance entirely. The astonishing culmination of this perceptual progress, of course, is when we open the "warped cover" of the book and read the inscription on the flyleaf, an activity that implies not only physical and emotional engagement with the scene but also a potentially disastrous disruption of the scene. The "glass bed-lamp," no longer safely propped on Hearn's tome, is left hovering in midair.

"Father's Bedroom" shows how a poem of modest discursive, perceptual, and philosophical proportions can do important work in those areas it seems to have conceded, precisely by seeming to have conceded them. It is, in the truest sense and in a sense that many more obviously "avant-garde" poems claim, an "experimental" poem. It experiments with genre, asking how few of its traditional constituents can be included in a poem and still have the poem count as an elegy; it experiments with tone, with poetic vision, and with discourse, seeking, in each of these cases, the minima that will suffice for poetic purposes.

A list-poem, then; but also, crucially, a poem about reading that comes to rest on an act of reading. Poems that undertake reading-acts are scarce elsewhere in lyric poetry: Wyatt's "Whoso List to Hunt" is perhaps the most famous example on a short list. In Lowell these kinds of poems are rather common, surprisingly so. When we read what Lowell reads—the inscription and reinscription on the flyleaf of the book—we do so simultaneously with Lowell.

> In the flyleaf:
> "Robbie from Mother."
> Years later in the same hand:
> "This book has had hard usage
> on the Yangtze River, China.
> It was left under an open
> porthole in a storm."
> (*Collected Poems* 177)

In a poem whose temporality is demarcated so carefully, it is important to note that our act of reading and his coincide. What the need to reinscribe the book shows, though, is that the permanence of writing depends on there being sturdy enough surfaces to write on: matter, here, is the master of spirit. Presumably if the book were left out again in a storm, Lowell's mother would again reinscribe it to account for the additional wear. But mothers live shorter lives than books, and so this particular act of writing is doomed. The inscription will be forgotten: like all such attempts to stop time, it will become a part of history. But by placing it into the sturdier temporality of artworks, Lowell has preserved, or sought to preserve, an incidental inscription on an incidental book. The great insight of this poem is to match Lowell's own sophisticated machinery for permanence—the continuity of lyric poetry itself—against his mother's cruder, doomed, attempt at permanence. Time and again throughout his poems Lowell will perform this function on written things, testing them against the permanence claimed anciently by poetry itself. The mother's inscription is only the simplest case in a category that includes national and civic mottoes, vows between friends and lovers, even the poet's own earlier words and poems. The status of readers and of written things in various contexts ("lyric," erotic, literary-historical, political) will come to be one of Lowell's richest topics.

Reading America

I mentioned Wyatt's sonnet "Whoso List to Hunt" above and want now to invoke it again to frame my discussion of Lowell's political poems. Here is the poem in its entirety:

> Whoso list to hunt, I know where is an hind,
> But as for me, alas, I may no more.
> The vain travail hath wearied me so sore,
> I am of them that farthest cometh behind.
> Yet may I by no means my wearied mind
> Draw from the deer, but as she fleeth afore
> Fainting I follow. I leave off therefore,
> Sithens in a net I seek to hold the wind.
> Who list her hunt, I put him out of doubt,
> As well as I may spend his time in vain.
> And graven with diamonds in letters plain
> There is written, her fair neck round about:
> *Noli me tangere*, for Caesar's I am,
> And wild for to hold, though I seem tame.
>   (Ferguson, Salter, and Stallworthy 113)

Ignoring many aspects of this poem, I want merely to point out its fascinating interrogation of political "possession" against competing claims. Those claims include the claims of the lover, drawn close enough to his beloved to see that she is unattainable, the citizen, brought near enough power to suffer its mystification (whether by kingly possession or by other means), and the poet,

whose own "net" of words at first seems to fail to "hold the wind."
And yet the poem, precisely by including the motto verbatim, asserts its own various means of "possession"—formal, perceptual,
discursive—as every bit as viable as Caesar's, and more permanent. (Ink—Shakespeare's "black ink"—being more permanent
than even the most durable matter, "diamonds," its durability
proved by precise comparison with hard matter like brass and
stone and precious matter like jewels.)

Like Wyatt, Lowell sees lyric poetry as an arena in which to
assert the claims of art against those of political power, often
by clarifying those claims. "Mouth of the Hudson" is one of
the many poems in *For the Union Dead* about the difficulty of
reading America as a sign. The book's central conceit is myopia,
which for Lowell signifies the inability to see into the common
world, the world constituted by what is beyond one's own body
and perhaps especially one's own books. That the myopic can see
the words on the page but nothing beyond them, nothing in the
world outside the window, suggests the difficulty of situating lyric
performance politically. The sensory crisis of myopia involves
taking the world nearest at hand, including the world of books,
as a viable substitute for the common world, as though reading
and living were synonymous. "Mouth of the Hudson" describes
several partially legible signs and the predicament they pose for
readers. Like the book in "Father's Bedroom," the litter along
the riverbank invites reading at perilously close range, reading
that disturbs the existing order of the scene. The poem begins
with an image of intense concentration, as "A single man stands
like a bird-watcher":

> A single man stands like a bird-watcher,
> and scuffles the pepper-and-salt snow
> from a discarded, gray
> Westinghouse Electric Cable Drum
> > (*Collected Poems* 328)

Already we can see that the legibility of this scene depends on our
disruption of it by scuffling away the layer of obfuscatory snow.

The kind of consolidated attention that a birdwatcher gives to a bird will not suffice here. The birdwatcher is a figure for distance and objectivity, since only by immersing himself quietly and distantly in the landscape will he glimpse the rare occurrence he expects. (This same principle of immersive absorption in the phenomenal world governs Lowell's many poems about fly-fishing, another activity in which humans try, in Jorie Graham's words, to "pass for the natural world.") But in this case perception is momentarily blocked by "pepper-and-salt snow" (itself a figure for the black and white of text) that we must clear in order for an act of reading to take place. These moments of staged reading are important, since they allegorize Lowell's own compositional process as well as our subsequent readerly process of uncovering the poem through time. Lowell reads the phrase "Westinghouse Electric Cable Drum" for the first time on the banks of the Hudson, then again as he types it out while composing the poem; every new reader of the poem shares these initial reading events in real time. The moment reminds us that lyric poetry means to immerse us so completely in the experience of reading that the ordinary distinction between reading and living breaks down.

And yet the poem informs us explicitly that reading is not a viable substitute for living. The man, Lowell says, "Cannot discover America by counting the chains of condemned freight trains from thirty states." Neither by reading their sides, then, or by "counting" them in metered verse, can we "discover America" (America being the only other proper name in the poem besides "Westinghouse"). The small-scale and personal act of reading, and by extension writing, poetry will not encompass the large fact of America, represented here by the figure of a "negro / [toasting] wheatseeds over a punctured barrel." The final illegibility of this scene, its resistance to discovery, and its implausibility as a metonymic substitution for "America" is suggested by the arresting image of ice "ticking seaward toward the Hudson / like the blank sides of a jigsaw puzzle." This enormously complex image presents the idea of time (as does the emphatic rhythm of the phrase "Westinghouse Electric Cable Drum" and the notion of counting freight trains). The geologic time of glaciers, the historic time of nations, the personal time of a single man's life, and the eternity of rivers coincide; the image also suggests that nature is an insoluble puzzle. The experience of living within all of these overlapping time frames is to be perpetually bewildered, like the man whose thwarted attempt to "discover America" has turned him into a birdwatcher, a connoisseur of small and picturesque events.

The wages of reading, of being a reader, are explored in Lowell's sonnet "Blizzard in Cambridge." If "Stopping by Woods on a Snowy Evening" is Frost's poem of the infinitely distended present, as snowflake after snowflake falls, Lowell's is a poem of snow having fallen. Like many of Lowell's sonnets, it is an exploration of the past participle, its relationship both to aesthetics and to ethics. Lowell's past-participial stance assumes a world already gathered into consequence before the poem's inception, or, if still forming, doing so one beat ahead of language and expression. It is up to other American poets (Stevens, Ammons, Ashbery), or this poet in other moods, to measure the ripening changes of the present in the present. The present participle has found its forms in our literature amply and (in Emerson and James and their expositors, Harold Bloom and Richard Poirier among others) found a theory to buttress those forms, but we haven't taken full measure, yet, of what it might feel like, what it might mean, to lag palpably a little behind phenomena—behind, even, our own insights and actions.

Here is "Blizzard in Cambridge":

Risen from the blindness of teaching to bright snow,
everything mechanical stopped dead,
taxis no-fares . . . the wheels grow hot from driving—
ice-eyelashes, in my spring coat; the subway
too jammed and late to wait for passengers;
snow trekking the mile from subway end to airport . . .
to all flights cancelled, fighting queues congealed
to telephones out of order, stamping buses,
rich, stranded New Yorkers staring with the wild, mild eyes
of steers at the foreign subway—then the train home,

jolting with stately grumbling: an hour in Providence,
in New Haven . . . the Bible. In darkness seeing
white arsenic numbers on the tail of a downed plane,
the smokestacks of abandoned fieldguns burning skyward.

(*Collected Poems* 559)

The state of having "risen from blindness" governs this poem,
its bafflement in the face of a world "congealed" into queues and
trains and miles while the interiors of a classroom, and a mind,
and indeed a poem sped forward. The only thing not slowed in
this poem is the poem itself, which moves headlong on itself,
clause upon clause propelled by the original force of the past
participle "risen." What the world undergoes while we tend to
the self is, of course, one of Lowell's richest topics, made richer
for his fear that self-maintenance involves not merely neglecting
the world, letting it go to seed, but actually inflicting violence on
it in one's absence, by means of one's absence. This is the great,
sorrowful topic of Lowell's poems about his institutionalization,
where self-maintenance requires setting up an alternate, paro-
distic home, with surrogates for one's children, one's wife, and
indeed oneself.

"Blindness" in the poem yields first to imperiled, partial sight,
as ones eyes adjust to the bright snow that makes everything too
near, then to the narcotized stare of the "steer"-like New Yorkers,
then to "the Bible," and finally to a miraculous act of reading,
in the darkness, "white arsenic numbers on the tail of a downed
plane." This inversion of ordinary text, where black letters are
stamped on white ground, suggests both the chalkboard of the
classroom and a photographic negative. But reading under adverse conditions—with one's glasses off, or with the text obscured
by snow, or by wear, or by water, or, as in this poem, in darkness—
is always in Lowell a figure for politics. What thwarted reading
represents, here and elsewhere, is the difficulty of inhabiting a
common world, a world legible to everyone. The failure of sight
means that we must operate only in the radically circumscribed
territory of the adjacent, the near-at-hand, and the private: that

the private life might constitute our only conceivable "master-piece," to borrow a phrase from Mark Strand—thus this poem, with its depiction of a city driven to sudden ruthlessness then angularity then resignation, individuals moving sluggishly through it, home. Or "Mouth of the Hudson," where a sequence of failed or partial acts of reading embodies the illegibility of an America that still systematically humiliates a portion of its citizens. In that poem, first we read the nonsensical but rhythmically invigorating name "Westinghouse Electric Drum" on the side of a discarded cable drum, then the names of states on the sides of "condemned freight trains" and finally the "wild ice ticking seaward down the Hudson / Like the blank sides of a jigsaw puzzle." These acts of thwarted or aborted reading won't allow us to "discover America," Lowell states, since the riverside detritus also includes "a Negro [toasting] wheat seeds over a punctured barrel." We can't interpret a common world, can't read its insignia intelligently, when so much of the text is deliberately mystified and when cruelty renders reading itself functionally beside the point.

What one ends up reading in "Blizzard in Cambridge" is, crucially, the "numbers on the tail of a downed plane," which when read rightly signify far beyond their mere denotative use. The poem was written in 1968; read backward from this penultimate image, the entire poem seems like an allegory for Vietnam and its sinister severing of people from their homes, many of those people the age of the students Lowell had been teaching at Harvard. We need the world at large, Lowell suggests, in order to read those numbers intelligently, and reading them intelligently means writing this poem, "Blizzard in Cambridge," a new text requiring new, straining readers. The act of straining to read, of reading in darkness, implies two things: first, the difficulty, or perhaps obscurity of the text, and second, the deliberate extension of the self in the interest of participating in a world beyond its boundaries. The gorgeous torrential energy of what is happening around us must, for a moment, be ignored, while these few figures, these few words, are summoned. But in the time it takes to read, a snow storm might well be happening—and by the time one rises, its having-happened, its existence in the past-participial form, of one's having risen into it from blindness, *is* the most immediate and urgent fact. Lowell's past participles, then, help us understand the wages of a life too exclusively interiorized or made real only as sense data or *epistemia*. It is not sense date or *epistemia* but, rather, snow and people that pile up in the time it takes to read "Blizzard in Cambridge."

Assigning to the poet the job of spelling out the national interest comes very near naming him prophet. But prophecy's conventional association with sight—the prophet communicates by means of "visions"—must be troubling to a poet who suffered from, and wrote frequently about, his own myopia. Lowell's "For the Union Dead" is his poem of myopic prophecy, an attempt to read America's past and future at absurdly close range. The usual vast sightlines of prophecy are here unavailable, as one after another of the poem's lenses is shown to be damaged or obscured. In its many images of ruptured or blocked sight it suggests that citizenship requires introspection but, also, involves forging for the near-at-hand world of one's own mind, one's own family, and one's own city, a viable inscription. The poem's epigraph is itself a revision of the existing inscription on the St. Gaudens Shaw Monument on the Boston Common: *Relinquunt Omnia Servare Rem Publicam*. The plural verb of Lowell's epigraph (*relinquunt*, "they gave up") revises the singular verb of St. Gaudens's original inscription (*reliquit*, "he gave up") implying, of course, that the heroism of the Massachusetts Fifty-fourth belonged not only to Robert Gould Shaw but to his regiment. But the act of revising an existing inscription, indeed one that is cast in bronze, seeks not to erase the original text but rather to add another layer of writing on top of it, to show how even the most permanent statements are subject to historical revision. Something of the history of race relations in our country can be gleaned merely by reading Lowell's epigraph in tandem with its original. The world of "For the Union Dead" is very much a world of crossings out and writings over, as many stages of historical time vie for the nearest and outermost plane of representation.

But this is as much a poem about reading as it is about writing, as its many images for reading and its cognates indicate. The poem begins with the same image for text that marked "Mouth of the Hudson":

> The old South Boston Aquarium stands
>   in a Sahara of snow now. Its broken windows are boarded.
> The bronze weathervane cod has lost half its scales.
> The airy tanks are dry.
>
> (Collected Poems 376)

We are again in the junked world of the city's outskirts, where signs seem to be shorn from their referents. The mingled snow and sand implied by the image of a "Sahara of snow" suggests, somehow, that the task this poem will set out to perform will be to read under adverse or obfuscatory conditions. The boarded windows imply damaged or compromised sight, recalling Lowell's many images of myopia. The impossibility of seeing through these windows opens, in the following stanza, an interior window into the private aquarium of one's past, where one's nose is perpetually pressed up against the glass:

> Once my nose crawled like a snail on the glass;
> my hand tingled
> to burst the bubbles
> drifting from the noses of the cowed, compliant fish.
>
> (Collected Poems 376)

This image is seen, crucially, from inside the aquarium; only from the point of view of the fish would Lowell's crushed nose look like a snail, and his hand seems to "tingle" toward us rather than away. The transparency of glass means that what we see sees us, in this case sees us engaged in an act of greedy, obsessive seeing. The nonchalance of the fish indicates their naturalness within the column of water called an aquarium, a nonchalance that will be brutally reconfigured as martial servitude, and then as slavery, later in the poem. This dream of transparency, where the self can see its objects and be seen seeing its objects, is never again realized in "For the Union Dead." As the poem progresses, we see through various blocked or obscured lenses: the chain link of a fence behind which "Yellow dinosaur steamshovels" operate; the orange scaffolding that obscures the statehouse; the bronze under which the black soldiers of the Fifty-fourth "seem to breathe"; the television set within which "the drained faces of Negro school children rise like balloons." These are all, of course, to some extent images for the text of the poem, which seems alternately like a fence, or like scaffolding, or like bronze, or like the pixelated screen of a TV.

Television offers us the awful privilege of watching people suffer at close range without any means of intervention. As such, it offers the poem's most important image of a damaged or ruptured lens. What Lowell sees very closely resembles what he once saw in the aquarium:

> When I crouch to my television set,
> the drained faces of Negro school-children rise like balloons.
> (*Collected Poems* 377)

What looking has come to involve, Lowell thinks, is ethical duty—but it is a duty that cannot be performed. We can no more live in the world of ray tubes and transistors than we can in the world of water, and both impossibilities suggest the impossible gap between Robert Lowell's Boston and the south (or, for that matter, South Boston) that systematically drains the life from its own children. Here, as in "Mouth of the Hudson," the attempt to read "America" at close range fails, since its signs are so far from their referents. The faces flashing on Lowell's TV set do so in Lowell's living room, but the children whom those faces describe are thousands of miles away and impossibly out of reach.

If this is a poem in part reflecting difficulties of writing and reading, it also, of course, reflects the inevitability of being written and being read. In all of the face-offs that the poem describes, both parties are accounted for—in all, that is, but one: the last. Previously, we have encountered man facing fish, man facing steam shovels, man facing monument, monument and statehouse facing each other, man and TV set facing each other. But in the final, startling stanza of the poem, "the aquarium" that held the world of objects at a safe, observable distance "is gone":

> The Aquarium is gone. Everywhere,
> giant finned cars nose forward like fish;
> a savage servility
> slides by on grease.
>
> (*Collected Poems* 377)

In a poem so dedicated to the careful delineation of its spatial terms (inside and outside, vertical and horizontal, background and foreground) so nearly dramaturgical in its insistence on exact spatial placement, the word "everywhere" is a shock—particularly so because in flooding its own representational plane, it renders itself pure object and allegorizes our point of view "outside" the aquarium-become-poem. We no longer see the world of fish and reptiles vicariously, through the eyes of a dramatic speaker who is hyperspecified in terms of time and place, but rather through our own eyes.

"Ones own must be learned as well as that which is foreign," writes Hölderlin (Schmidt). Crucially, what Lowell can't see well, or can't see consistently, or can only see in "flashes and specks" is "his own" Boston; Colonel Shaw is his ancestor, and the Public Garden, the statehouse, the Common are all monuments of municipal and national significance but also elements of Lowell's finely wrought personal iconography. The discovery of oneself already present in the world, already implicated—and rather unflatteringly—in history, is among Lowell's deepest subjects. He claims for himself no transcendence; he wants Whitmanian largeness without the clemency Whitman's largeness grants him. If Whitman is always "Beginning from Paumanok," Lowell is always, at every stage in his career, somberly concluding a narrative that began long before his appearance here but that anticipated him all along.

Elizabeth Bishop on Autobiographical Grounds

Scrutiny: "Poem"

It has become a commonplace to describe Elizabeth Bishop not in terms of what she said but what she should have said. The placid surface of her poems conceals a severe and variegated subaqueous terrain; her famous "reticence" suggests an unwillingness to be candid. That she suffered immensely (as a severe asthmatic, as an alcoholic, as an orphan, as a lesbian) and was, as she told Robert Lowell, "the loneliest person who ever lived" (*One Art* 360): these facts about Bishop's life, though well known, are by and large absent from her work, which, set beside Lowell's or Anne Sexton's or John Berryman's, seems reserved and cryptic, even self-protective. The sense of an individuated person, so strong in Bishop, arises from her scrupulous detail, her fierce and luminous accuracy, her unusual angles and points of view: her eccentricity is often precisely literal, aligned with oblique perception, with the "Man-Moth" who rides the subway facing backward or with "The Unbeliever" who sleeps, and dreams "at the top of the mast." The angles are no less oblique when the subject matter is explicitly "autobiographical," as it comes more frequently to be later in Bishop's career. Bishop's autobiographical accuracy, unlike Lowell's or Frank O'Hara's, depends on taking strenuously novel perspectives. As many critics have shown, hers is an art of relation, of perceptual nuance, of points of view, rather than an art of factual substantiation.

But as I will argue in this chapter, Bishop's later poems are no more "candid" or "revealing" than her early poems of veiled identity. If they tend to be staged close to home, on familiar autobiographical grounds, it is often precisely to unsteady our command of terms like "home" and "autobiographical." Often finding herself at home only locates her more irretrievably in a work of art, as in her famous poem "Poem," which scrutinizes a watercolor painting of one of her childhood homes ("About the size of an old-style dollar bill").

"Poem" is a important source for understanding Bishop's ideas about art's relationship to personal experience, in part because it makes autobiography adapt to an unusual scale, in part because of her strong, abashed identification with sentimental artists and works of art. A watercolorist herself, it is likely she thought even of her own paintings as workings out, in other terms, of the problems posed by her poems. Bishop's watercolors display her resolve to be, in her creation of artifacts, "homemade": the less sublime the painting, the more likely it is to express authentic sensibility. And so with the small painting in "Poem." It is a mark of Bishop's poise in relation to autobiographical topics that she would represent the self as, though heirloom-like (that is to say, "cherished" and "significant"), still nevertheless "useless and free . . . handed along collaterally to owners / who looked at it sometimes, or didn't bother to." The painting's diminutive scale raises the possibility, furthermore, that it may not be a finished painting at all, but merely a "sketch for a larger one." This presents the notion of a lost, even conjectural, original for which the significant objects in a life, heirlooms and such, stand in, but in doing so reveal their own inadequacy. The painting's tiny size makes it by nature a site of nostalgia, a kind of orphaned object bearing an eerie resemblance to its absent parents, but it also makes it dismissible, a "minor family relic," perhaps a mere curiosity. It is one of the "homemade" contraptions that so interest Bishop throughout her career, objects that seem somehow to bear the traces of their maker's peculiar wishes. We are never very far, in "Poem," from the desire of an artist (Bishop's great-uncle, as we eventually learn) to render a scene expertly, never far from the idea of an artist's circumscribed and limited "mere expertise," or, to use Bishop's word, his "specialty":

> Elm trees, low hills, a thin church steeple
> —that gray-blue wisp—or is it? In the foreground
> a water meadow with some tiny cows,
> two brushstrokes each, but confidently cows;
> two minuscule white geese in the blue water,
> back-to-back, feeding, and a slanting stick.
> Up closer, a wild iris, white and yellow,
> fresh-squiggled from the tube.
> The air is fresh and cold; cold early spring
> clear as gray glass; a half-inch of blue sky
> below the steel-gray storm clouds.
> (They were the artist's specialty.)
> A specklike bird is flying to the left.
> Or is it a flyspeck looking like a bird?
>
> (*Poems* 176)

"It must be Nova Scotia," Bishop conjectures. But she can make only momentary gains in her desire to see the place as in any sense real, since the means of depiction—paint squiggles and brushstrokes—so insistently intervene. The painting seems almost to be reaching out from the surface of its canvas toward the tip of a brush, the brush toward a hand, the hand toward her great-uncle, now long dead; the painting records not a place called Nova Scotia but rather a sensibility, or what Bishop later calls "a look." The difficulty of treating the painting as a real thing (where real means "a depiction of Nova Scotia") is compounded by its insoluble materiality, not only its minute size but also its hardness, its susceptibility to the litter of a fly's smashed body.

The strange status of this little painting within the idea of art—the problems its size, its provenance, its style, its materiality pose to its reception as an aesthetic object—create Bishop's state of attention, that is to say not only her angle of attention but also the kind of attention, the kind of scrutiny, she must lend to it. The self shown to be temporarily recoverable in the painting is not really rendered by its squiggles and brushstrokes but, rather, under them—and the act of recovery involves not just careful attention but resourceful, imaginative attention. Bishop must look very hard at the painting in order to see through it to a place she "recognizes," but she must also involve herself, almost ally herself, with its particular manner of seeing. The work of seeing Nova Scotia is work begun by her great-uncle but completed by Bishop, and the sight of the place leads to a discovery of the self within it. The intervening moment of self-recognition is, therefore, an experience of sudden transparency, as though the painting became, for a moment anyway, a window on an actual scene:

> Heavens, I recognize the place, I know it!
> It's behind—I can almost remember the farmer's name.
> His barn backed on that meadow.
>
> *(Poems* 177)

The sense here is that the self is not something one comes upon in a landscape but rather a way of seeing that landscape at an emotionally consequential angle. We can suddenly see across the meadow depicted in the painting to the back of a farmer's barn, a farmer whose name is also tantalizingly outside the frame. It is as though an old, lost cell were spliced into the filmstrip that constitutes ongoing perception, but one cell and one cell only—and so before long we are back in the present tense, scrutinizing the material object, the painting in our hands

>   There it is,
> titanium white, one dab. The hint of steeple,
> filaments of brush-hairs, barely there,
> must be the Presbyterian church.
> Would that be Miss Gillespie's house?
> Those particular geese and cows
> are naturally before my time.
>
> *(Poems* 177)

This is the moment of focusing the binoculars or of wiping the fog off of a window that will not stay clear. The means of sight, the interface, keeps dissolving and reforming in the foreground of perception, perhaps like a curtain that billows and settles, billows and settles, in front of the window. This experience of losing and regaining focus calls attention to the process of seeing, the means by which we "see" through the surface of a painting to the scene it portrays. The act of seeing is suddenly inextricable from the idea of seeing, the theoretics of seeing, and so Bishop has occasion to step back from the objects of perception and consider them in the abstract. The "coincidence" as Bishop calls it, later, of "two looks" "collaps[es] life and the memory of it." Bishop can suddenly see what her great-uncle saw and, in doing so, see what she saw through her own eyes; the poem ends with a catalog of the scene:

> . . . the munching cows,
> the iris, crisp and shivering, the water
> still standing from spring freshets,
> the yet-to-be-dismantled elms, the geese.
> (*Poems* 177)

"Poem," as its title suggests, is a self-conscious artifact, aware not only of its own angles of sight but of ours. The concluding catalog is ingenious in that it finds a way of making us see through its own act of seeing, as well as through the artist's way of seeing, to the archetypally simple scene it describes. "By the end of the poem," writes Helen Vendler, "the poet has united herself with the artist" (*Part* 104). Every new reader of "Poem" is taught, in the course of reading the poem, how seeing things freshly depends on seeing them rigorously, as the events that make up the activity called "sight" are slowed down, isolated, and identified. But "seeing" in the poem is not, finally, the point; the poem is not about perception any more than, say, "After Apple Picking" is about apple picking. Or to put it more accurately, "Poem" is about seeing just as "After Apple Picking" is about apple picking precisely to the degree that seeing, and apple picking, are human activities that instruct the self in the conditions that formed it. In particular "Poem" is about finding the self through objective circumstances, among them an heirloom miniature painting and the barns and geese and farmers it depicts; these are the subcellular units, so to speak, of emotional life.

Reading "Poem" as an allegory (as it insists we do) for poetry's role in the recovery of missing bits of the self, we might isolate the following stages or processes of that recovery. First, the art object (poem or painting) is likely to obscure exactly to the degree to which, and just in the place where, it seems most to clarify. It is "always true," as David Ferry writes, that in lyric poetry "our vivid consciousness of the artifice of its forms makes is vividly, radiantly conscious of our experience of its meanings" (Ferry xiv). But Bishop's self-conscious focusing and refocusing, her interest not only in the painted scene but in its paintedness, its material elements, ask us to be vividly conscious of the way artifacts are assembled, to imagine the painting as an end result of a process whose name it shares. There are no transparent poems, since poetry is life lived (as R. P. Blackmur says) "at the remove of form and meaning" (4). What is ours and ours alone must always be excavated in language by means of language. Bishop, an orphan, knew that we are all orphans within language, waking into a household whose rules and structures both compensate us for loss and refer, perpetually, to our condition. While the essential, even traumatic events of childhood are happening to us we are surrounded by a world blithely unaware of us. We therefore cannot help but have known the cows and elms and irises at the end of "Poem," and their inevitability lends them their autobiographical charge.

Second, "recognizing" the scene means that the speaker must find herself within it, and doing so depends on looking at it very closely, so closely that she must surrender the consolations of distance entirely. "The world has wonderful details if you can get it just a little closer than usual," Bishop wrote to Anny Baumann, her doctor, who had given her a gift of binoculars. The act of looking closely is synonymous, in Bishop, with self-surrender, since close scrutiny involves relinquishing one's usual, socially conditioned ways of seeing. (Bishop's interest in optical devices like binoculars issues not only from the access to beauty they provide but also from the way they require us to make our selves entirely contiguous with sight, rendering all other aspects of the self temporarily inaccessible.) Bishop had always found, on looking closely, arrangements that seemed emotionally, even morally, suggestive; she "loved mold and mildew" not for their abstract beauty but rather for their insinuatingly human-seeming involvements. But as "Poem" demonstrates, the self can be literally located in what seems, on first inspection, foreign and peripheral. It is as though the painting somehow included Bishop all this time, even while moldering in an old trunk. Her inclusion in the painting, despite her and unbeknownst to her, figures our own inclusion in "Poem" as readers who come on it and its requirements of us late, as it were. This expectation of optical and imaginative flushness requires that we, too, train our vision on the miniature object in our hands.

This expectation of unusually close scrutiny distinguishes Bishop's autobiographical poems from those in the "confessional" mode. "This suffering business," Bishop called confessional poetry: "You wish they would keep some of these things to themselves" (Kalstone 112). Confessionality seemed to require, as one of its presiding fictions, theatricality; the reader's role in a Sexton poem is to maintain a kind of shocked or sympathetic quietude outside the bounds of the poem. Bishop's antitheatrical desire to conceal or encrypt the personal life has been read as a sign either of her own primness or her inability, given society's primness, to tell her transgressive story plainly and clearly. But as I read it, Bishop's reticence is a way of making a work of art that, like the little heirloom painting in "Poem," asks us to try very hard to see it for what it is, perhaps even to align our angle of vision with its own. "Watch it closely," Bishop warns us at the close of "The Monument," a poem that demonstrates the necessity, despite seemingly diminishing returns, of keeping our eyes trained on detail. It is impossible, in "The Monument," to perform the demanded act of "seeing" the object in question; its manifold, exfoliating aspects are presented serially, and each new aspect seems to erase the old ones. But "seeing the monument" is not particularly the point; the point is rather to create a kind of attention, a state of watching, of being enthralled and expectant.

Third, poetry is normatively sincere, even painfully or embarrassingly so—even, at times, sentimental. The painting in "Poem" is nothing if not lovingly rendered, and therefore touchingly, compellingly inadequate as art. The doilies and decorative displays of oil cans that brighten a little filling station are, likewise, evidence of, and occasion for, sentimentality:

> Somebody embroidered the doily.
> Somebody waters the plant,
> or oils it, maybe. Somebody
> arranges the rows of cans
> so that they softly say:
> ES—SO—SO—SO
> to high-strung automobiles.
> Somebody loves us all.
>
> (*Poems* 128)

These little stays against confusion carry none of the existential gravitas of Frost's crumbling stone walls and empty foundations, but Bishop, like Frost, is interested in the status of axioms and adagios in a dynamic, mutable world. "Filling Station" can be seen as an experiment in sentimentality, an attempt to render the world viably by sentimental means. It takes an adequately "oil-soaked, oil-permeated" place to make the presence of doilies, or the presence of statements like "Somebody loves us all," sufficiently astringent to count among the constituents of a lyric poem.

Bishop's spectacles of kindness, of good intentions, mark her as temperamentally distinct from Lowell and Berryman, but they do not make her ultimately or simply (or dismissibly) an optimist. Cheerfulness, after all, is a part of the world. But the sentimental excesses of Bishop's rhetoric contribute, further, to the status of her poems as homemade objects. "The Monument," the heir-loom painting in "Poem," and the flute Crusoe plays to pass the time in "Crusoe in England" are all homemade things, and it is the kind of attention that homemade things require of us, the ways homemade artworks involve us, that will be my primary focus in this chapter. Hugh Kenner's book *A Homemade World* identified one strain, within modernism, of linguistic artifact that sought to master experience (figured as dizzyingly complex and scurryingly evasive) by technological means. (This effect is the one Jarrell lamented when he called William Carlos Williams's worse poems "winning machine parts minus their machines.") Williams's and George Oppen's miniatures, Marianne Moore's precision, Ernest Hemingway's tight syntax all seem like aesthetic contraptions, ingenious and a little sad. Joseph Cornell's boxes, which Bishop loved, constitute another example of this aesthetics of the homemade, by which a specified self can be made radi-antly present not by means of self-portraiture but rather through eccentricities of tone, scale, and proportion. Both Cornell and Bishop seek to embody in individual works of art traces of the particularity, not to say peculiarity, of individual selves. Bishop finds the use of personae especially effective in conveying sen-sibility and in making sensibility the sine qua non of selfhood. Like O'Hara she is most herself when weighing in and exclaim-ing, and she often, like him, finds herself taken aback. The kind of poem Bishop writes will not bear facticity, either Lowell's kind or O'Hara's. Rather, in Bishop we find the self present in a kind of expressive homeliness and naïveté, a stance whose repre-sentational parameters are as rigid and narrow, in their way, as the parameters of Cornell's boxes. Identity is not, as in Lowell and O'Hara, something one carries along with oneself, burden or talisman or luck charm but, rather, whatever one finds near at hand and tries on, marveling at the fit. Like her depilated, mal-nourished "Pink Dog" walking the streets of Rio during carnival, Bishop finds not only solace but also protection in disguise.

"The painting-poem," writes Robert Pinsky in *The Situa-tion of Poetry*, "is a distinct contemporary genre, and one of the commonplaces of that genre consists in linking the idea of craft with the idea of reticence or indirection" (Pinsky 106)." "Poem" is a painting poem, though, which argues that the cool eye of the painter is insufficient for accurate sight. The poem asks us to consider a painting that not only requires scrutiny but asks, furthermore, to be held in our hands. There is no way of seeing it without finally seeing our place in it; and such close scrutiny cannot but blind us, temporarily, to everything outside its frame. Its consolations are not those of "high art" or the sublime but, rather, those of homemade things, things to which everyone would apply the words "sincere" and "authentic" and "touching." Bishop's poems are unmistakably art, and she believes profoundly in the sublime, but still for their proportions, their intimacy of tone, and their sincerity, these poems constitute a critique of "reticence" and artistic coolness, without swinging to the other pole and embracing confessionalism. For this reason, Bishop's poems make us think harder about the limits and limitations of autobiography than any others in our period.

Narrative: "Sestina," "The Moose"

When Bishop speaks, in "Poem," of "life and the memory of it so compressed / they've turned into each other," she is identifying one solution to a problem that concerns her throughout her career, namely, the problem of narrative. Bishop's is a vexed attraction to the conventions of narrative, and her poems frequently seem to be seeking alternatives to the narrative's deterministic governance of phenomena and its habitual unexamined faith in causality. Unlike Lowell, with his impressionistic Freudianism, Bishop is largely incurious in the world of childhood as a site of first causes and principles; her poems about childhood seem, like her vision of little Arthur in "First Death in Nova Scotia," frozen in a state of sensory pungency and immediacy. In that poem (as frequently in Bishop) the potential for interpretive retrieval is negated, in advance, by her choosing to see the child's world through the child's eyes. Her ideal is the icon, which is able to present all the elements of a narrative at once, outside of time. In "The Roosters" she describes how, in a medieval sculpture of Saint Peter's denial of Jesus, the whole story and its verbal summary could be "set in one small scene, past and future":

> Christ stands amazed,
> Peter, two fingers raised
> to surprised lips, both as if dazed.
>
> But in between
> a little cock is seen
> carved on a dim column in the travertine,
>
> explained by *gallus canit*,
> *flet Petrus* underneath it.
>
> (*Poems* 38)

This fantasy of representational simultaneity presents a world where, as Bishop says in "Five Flights Up," "everything is answered, / all taken care of, / no need to ask again." It is in the nature of Jesus to be denied, of Peter to do the denying, and of the rooster, whose cry signifies time, to preside over the whole sad business. There is nothing to be learned from the story, no "moral," no room for remorse or repentance, and if the same elements were aligned again there would be the same results. The story, such as it is, is already a redundancy.

In Bishop's "Sestina" this desire to be an icon is partially realized as the raw ingredients of a "comforting" autobiographical narrative become the end terms, the elements, of one of the strangest and most formally complex English verse forms. Bishop had written an earlier sestina, "A Miracle for Breakfast," as "a kind of stunt" (Kalstone 109). That poem uses the structural intricacies, the displacements and replacements native to the sestina form, to chart how a "hard crumb" became a many-chambered "beautiful villa" for the pauper whose meager breakfast it had been. The poem is not, to my mind, entirely successful—its fairytale atmospherics seem a little desperate and eager-to-please— but it does establish the link, in Bishop, between the ordinary economies of domestic life (how is breakfast made? what should we do in lieu of breakfast?) and the uncanny economies, the "miracles" of transformation that art promises.

"Sestina" is comparatively grimmer about the prospect of miraculous transport. In "Sestina," the scene is radically "a grandmother's kitchen"; the poem has eliminated in advance the option of miraculous escape. The repeated ingredients—"house," "grandmother," "child," "stove," "almanac," "tears"—suggest at once the impoverishment of autobiographical fact and the inevitability of our return to it, no matter how poor and quaint it seems. The alphabet-like simplicity and rigidity of childhood provide the substantive content of memory, memory that must somehow, despite its few, stiff constituents, govern the intricate and perplexing forms of later life. The passage of these elements is traced in the poem through a kind of ecosystem of the imagination, each element expending itself only to reappear, transformed and seemingly redeemed, in the next stanza. This process of incorporation and reincorporation would seem to suggest an infinite series of stanzas (or a series of stanzas whose repetitiveness was so marked that it came to seem, to the reader, to be infinite) until, that is, the process of substitution and reconfiguration is suddenly halted, compressed, and frozen in the final stanza:

> *Time to plant tears*, says the almanac.
> The grandmother sings to the marvelous stove
> and the child draws another inscrutable house.
>
> (*Poems* 124)

And another, and another—the poem suggests an open set where houses could be "drawn" ad infinitum, and where every house "drawn" would be inscrutable. The dynamic processes of childhood, the tea brewing and being poured, the moons rising and falling, the grandmother singing become suddenly fixed and static; it is in the nature of such frozen events in time to raise the question of their own scrutability, their interpretive value—or as we more colloquially say, their "meaning." Bishop raises the issue of meaning without restricting it to any one conundrum or proposing any one solution. The visual arts provide her with a model of how to do so, here and elsewhere. But the house and indeed all the other elements of this little scene are "inscrutable" because we live in them, so to speak; the "child" who draws is as determined and fixed a part of the total structure of the poem, as necessary a part of its design, as the house that she draws. "Scrutability" depends on an objective point of view, a point of view outside of the house one is attempting to scrutinize. We can draw our "inscrutable" houses only within other, larger inscrutable houses; the language we use is made from the cloth of the phenomenon it purports to interpret.

"Sestina" is too generalized and estranged to be considered an "autobiographical" poem even in the thwarted sense of some of Bishop's other poems, but it is a poem with a polemical interest in autobiography. The displacements of the sestina function, like the alphabetical arrangement of Roland Barthes's *Roland Barthes by Roland Barthes*, to "banish every origin" and to "halt, to deflect, to divide" the self from an inevitable teleological career (Anderson 70). Its formal claustrophobia corresponds to what Bishop feels being immersed in the rote and shopworn facts of lived life. Only the severe architecture of the sestina can wring from these emblems of the cherished and personal a sense of the real, but the extreme artifice of the representational means exacts a very high price. The astonishing thing about "Sestina" is that it constitutes the most transparent, the most emotionally and cognitively immediate, solution to a representational problem, namely, how to render the arbitrary design at the bottom of selfhood. But the poem still seems mournful about its representational choices, as though it wished to be a Wordsworthian recovery of the exact hues and pitches of childhood, not this odd surreal brocade.

It is possible to see a poem like "Sestina" as an evasion, beautiful indeed but true only so far as it goes. Like Marianne Moore, Bishop is supposed to have perfected a way of making perfection itself seem emotionally freighted, as though it took heroic courage not to say what was on one's mind. Bishop's preference for the mirror of worldly exactitude over the lamp of subjective expressivity is seen, furthermore, against the backdrop of a certain historical moment whose conditions conspired to make it desirable and advantageous for some people (principally men) to speak their minds, where others were silenced. Adrienne Rich has argued that these strictures forced Bishop to map the transgressive material of her "intimate" life onto eroticized narratives of cultural difference: "Poems examining intimate relationships are almost wholly absent from Bishop's later work. What takes their place is a series of poems examining relationships between people who are, for reasons of difference, distanced: rich and poor, landlord and tenant, white man and black man, invader and native" (Rich 18). Rich will not say what might constitute an "examination" of "intimate relationships" or, for that matter, what kind of "intimate relationship" she has in mind. And while it might be said that Bishop's Brazilian poems display a slight naïveté about difference and that her subjects, in those poems, too often seem benignly and quaintly "foreign," no one could read those poems as "examinations" of cultural power. Rich's hypothesis, though plausible in the abstract, misses the tenor and pitch of Bishop's poems, their really intimate tones and proportions.

Rich's impulse to see the intimate life as both present in and absent from Bishop's work is a correct one, though. This effect arises, I would suggest, partly from her notion of herself as essentially "insignificant" (a notion mentioned in my chapter on Lowell) and partly from her distrust of narrative itself, personal narrative not excepted. On reading Lowell's poem "Fall 1961" (in which a grandfather clock figures importantly), Bishop writes: "Your poem is haunting me—I find I have it almost memorized. We had a clock that had a ship that rocked back and forth, and another one that showed something moving on the window of the house on a green hill—I always thought it was someone shaking out the sheets" (Kalstone 209–10). Lowell's poem is loaded with Freud, as the phallic clock looms over the domestic scene; indeed, in a vignette that recurs several times in Lowell's work, the young poet knocks his father down and causes him to hit his head on such a clock. The clock is also, as the poem makes clear, an image for the state and for the precariousness and doom of the Cold War. But for Bishop the clock is more like a Cornell box or like the little painting in "Poem," bearing in its body, clumsily but poignantly, a glimpse of Nova Scotia. This insistent seeing-through (even through the mahogany and brass of Lowell's style) functions to retrieve a fragile, an immensely imperiled gesture itself inscribed on the surface of a glass window, "someone shaking out the sheets." Lowell's poem is about the scowl of time, especially as the ticking away of time, in the Cold War, takes on a kind of cartoon menace. "Fall 1961" is a terrified and a terrifying poem, entirely characteristic of Lowell; it is therefore remarkable that Bishop could find what she does inscribed on its face.

The imperiled status of a landscape or a gesture within time is related to the status of incidents within narrative, narrative that seems to require a kind of eventfulness as its fuel. In a normative autobiographical narrative, we would proceed from station to station, each one describing an event in the narrator's life, all of them (taken together) accounting for the formation of a unique personality. It matters little whether these events are related more or less chronologically, as in Augustine and Rousseau and Wordsworth, or, as in a Freudian narrative like Lowell's, in order of their revelation in the consciousness. The point is that narrative itself, with its almost martial drive forward, then forward again, insists on the evidentiary cash value of specific events in relation to an overall argument. Events are the buttresses of narrative, autobiographical narrative included. Bishop's notion of her own insignificance, then, makes autobiographical narrative a practical impossibility. The determinism of narrative, the sense of life as lining up inevitably and agreeably under its influence, often seems to Bishop irretrievable to art. The aesthetic strategies for conjuring the Uncle Arties of the world differ from those of conjuring the Uncle Devereux Winslows. Lowell's manner—remorseful, tending on the one hand to passivity or, on the other hand, toward violent outburst—is that of a character who finds himself born on page 450 of a 500-page novel. Bishop's narrative is precisely her narrative poverty, her sense of having been picked up and placed arbitrarily in the world.

The image of "someone shaking out the sheets" that Bishop recalls in the light of "Fall 1961" reappears in her late poem "The Moose." There, the image of "a woman shaking a tablecloth / out after supper" is one of the many sights one sees on a long overnight bus trip south. "The Moose" is not obviously an auto-biographical poem, but it is, obviously and insistently, a narrative one. It describes a trip from Nova Scotia to Boston, a trip on narrow roads, past salt marshes, and through dark woods, which lend to it the feeling of radical linearity. The poem is carried forward syntactically by an astonishing opening sentence that covers thirty-six lines and six stanzas. The stanzas create the sensation of rest, of "stops" on a long bus trip, while the forward thrust of this single sentence keeps us from seeing too much of any one sight, however beautiful or poignant. The quietly emphatic trimeters (which she derived from Carlos Drummond de Andrade, the Brazilian poet) function as a kind of internal timepiece, as the landscape ticks away, receding into what we call "the past" even as they exist, perpetually, in a timeless present of their own. The bus travels, we are told,

> down hollows, up rises,
> and waits, patient, while
> a lone traveler gives
> kisses and embraces
> to seven relatives
> and a collie supervises.
>   (*Poems* 172)

One by one these lone travelers step into the element of time, which carries each of them forward, through the night, to a common destination. The roadside world is seen precisely, noted

as though for the last time; even the most transitory and delicate
gesture attains, in this light, the condition of permanence:

> . . . the sweet peas cling
> to their wet white string
> on the whitewashed fences;
> bumblebees creep
> inside the foxgloves,
> and evening commences.
> (*Poems* 172)

The iconic permanence of sculpture, which Bishop describes in
"The Roosters" and enacts in "Sestina," is here heightened by the
fact of our moving inexorably forward, forward, unable to dwell
in any one place any longer than a moment. It is the very capacity
of the bumblebees and collies to exist seemingly outside of time
that forces the consciousness of time on us. These emblematic
scenes are only emblematic from our point of view; from the
collie's point of view, or that of the bumblebees, it is perhaps the
passing busses, one a night for years, which attain the condition
of permanence.

In its movement forward and away from points of origin, then,
the bus is a figure for narrative—if only insofar as narrative is itself a figure for the passage of time and the certainty of human
mortality within time. In the little allegory of "The Moose," the
bus trip, unlike the heroic journeys of Dante or Odysseus, is to-
tally arbitrary, with a fixed point of origin and a fixed destination
but no compelling reason for moving from point A to point B.
Boston is simply where we travel to when the bus arrives, the bus
that waits on us until we have said our proper good-byes. The
bus, its flanks bleached and pitted, is of course a kind of body, as
is the road, which a bridge "rattles / but doesn't give way." The
bus, the body, travels its own course, regardless of its passengers,
whose reasons for travel are in the final tally irrelevant. This is
not a quest poem; the bus will turn around and drive back to
Nova Scotia.

The bus, since it has in its very body a front, a middle, and a back comes itself to be (like the road it travels) an image for time, with the "oldest" people, sitting in the back, in the dark. Their voices can be heard, like voices in our memories, "Grandparents' voices"; but there is no way they can be seen, and anyway their conversation, Bishop says, is "not concerning us":

> In the creakings and noises,
> an old conversation
> —not concerning us,
> but recognizable, somewhere,
> back in the bus:
> Grandparents' voices
>
> uninterruptedly
> talking, in Eternity:
> names being mentioned,
> things cleared up finally . . .
> (*Poems* 172)

In the dark, in the hushed tones of nighttime conversation, among the "creakings and noises" of the road and the bus, conversation is shorn off from specific referents, and what Frost calls "the sound of sense" prevails. These vocal stiffenings and loosenings, speedings-up and slowings-down, are the product of the voice fastening itself to urgent, intimate matters, but the tonal contour of this information is common and communicable; the disclosures that follow are generalized enough to be anyone's, then, which means they might as well belong, perhaps do belong, to Bishop:

> what he said, what she said,
> who got pensioned;
>
> deaths, deaths and sicknesses;
> the year he remarried;
> the year (something) happened.
> She died in childbirth.
> That was the son lost
> when the schooner foundered.

He took to drink. Yes.
She went to the bad.
When Amos began to pray
even in the store and

finally the family had
to put him away.
              (*Poems* 172)

Though located "in the back of the bus" these statements in indirect discourse are as "direct" and transparent as any in the poem. The flaw in reportage represented by the word "something" lends to them a kind of wide applicability, as though they became true of anyone who found himself speaking them. They seem to have their own objective and noncontingent existence in the world, like letters of the alphabet, and they become meaningful and true only in combination. These are the elemental events in anyone's life, statements that claim everyone as their potential subjects and predicates, which is why the conversation seems to happen "in Eternity."

But recollection (and perhaps therefore the eternity where it seems to unfold) is, as the poem teaches us, itself temporally fixed, an act that happens in time. The tender and sad retrospection of this conversation happens in a bus that moves, despite its backward glance, inexorably forward. The conceit of the bus trip solves Bishop's problem of "insignificance," since it allows her to overhear the tones of sincere recollection, as though they were none of hers, but nevertheless present them in primary position, as though they were hers; it solves the problem of narrative by showing how every narrative rests on another narrative, the passenger on the bus on the road and so on and so on. These elements of the poem function as critiques of "mastery," to use Costello's phrase, and therefore of aesthetic finish. The poem keeps us from feeling (as in the title of a recent Mark Strand poem) that "Our Masterpiece Is the Private Life." Even to embed these recollective acts in the larger recollective narrative of the poem is to undermine the notions of authorship and mastery on which autobiographical narratives are founded. But the most important critique of narrative happens not just in "The Moose," but to the moose, and that is the "screeching halt" occasioned by the moose's appearance. The placement of this event in the poem is notable. We have just been told that "Now, it's all right now / even to fall asleep / just as on all those nights." Though the entire poem has taken place in the present tense, it is only now that the present has (in a phrase of William James's) "sensible duration." The word "now" has, up to this point, been notably absent, as though it were too fugitive to be named. The poem's sense of the present had been of sudden, jarring eventfulness, a dog's single bark, or the time it takes a "brisk" elderly lady to make her way from the bus door to her seat. But suddenly, with the repetition of that word "now," we are in an element that allows for contemplation and that promises an opiate calm. The sudden arrival of the moose, then, disturbs not just the narrative momentum of the poem but also the narcotic perfection of the moment:

> —Suddenly the bus driver
> stops with a jolt,
> turns off his lights.
>
> A moose has come out of
> the impenetrable wood
> and stands there, looms, rather,
> in the middle of the road.
> It approaches; it sniffs at
> the bus's hot hood.
>
> (*Poems* 172)

The appearance of the moose happens simultaneously to the bus and to the poem, causing us to feel, along with Bishop and the other passengers, a "sweet sensation of joy." "We *all* feel this," as Bishop says. The untranslatability of the moose into language accounts for the slackness of that phrase ("sweet sensation of joy"), which is moving precisely to the degree that it does not venture more complex visual or linguistic mastery. Indeed the entire passage evinces a linguistic insufficiency that, while utterly appropriate to the experience of sudden fear or sudden joy, suggests furthermore the limits of narrative description. The most significant events, Bishop seems to argue, are destined to remain outside the scope of description. It is perhaps their very status as excessive or fugitive that makes them, in the end, significant. A poet who believes such things will not arrive uncomplicatedly at self-description.

One Kind of Everything: "Crusoe in England"

The question of what counts as autobiography in Bishop cannot be answered without considering her late narrative poem "Crusoe in England," surely one of the strangest autobiographical poems ever written. To begin with, the poem is the autobiography not of Bishop but of Robinson Crusoe; but this Crusoe has access to so many of Bishop's unmistakable mannerisms that the poem becomes not only "about" the real Bishop but about the way we read autobiographical poems and about how poems can be said to refer to the lives of their makers. It is a poem, I take it, about confessionality, in a way that other more "confessional" poems could never be; it holds the idea of autobiography up for inspection, even while serving, oddly, as the most intimate and affecting of autobiographies. Along with "Ulysses and Circe," Robert Lowell's exquisite late poem, it constitutes the most profound assessment of the prestige of autobiographical fact to be written in our period. Both of these poems seem to be written out of a kind of beautiful fatigue regarding the conventions of self-representation, especially the conventions that underwrite candor and sincerity. Lowell had told us much about his life by the time of "Ulysses and Circe"; Bishop had told us little but had mastered a tone of sincerity and poignancy that served an autobiographical function. But when the self ceases to be a dynamic process and becomes a fixed object—when, to use Stevens's terms, "the planet" is "on the table"—poetry can come to seem like stenography, meekly reliant on the actual. In part,

"Crusoe in England" is an attempt to unfix the tones of recollection and self-scrutiny (or "self-pity" as Bishop calls it in the poem) from their reliance on autobiographical narrative. These poems may be loosely called "antimythical" or "antiheroic," but that description sounds thin in the telling. "Crusoe in England" and "Ulysses and Circe" have no interest in whether we live in mythic times or sadly fallen and desecrated ones; the old categories of high and low, mythic and quotidian, are beside the point. The question is how one's own life comes to seem to oneself "mythic," meaning among other things "common to everyone" and "insufficiently individuated"—and thereby alien, strange, uncanny. By the time of the publication of "Crusoe in England" there are two "Elizabeth Bishops," just as in Borges's prose poem there are two Borgeses, "Borges and I": "It is Borges, the other one, that things happen to. I walk through Buenos Aires and I pause—mechanically now, perhaps—to gaze at the arch of an entryway and its inner door; news of Borges reaches me by mail, or I see his name on a list of academics or in some biographical dictionary" (278). One way of thinking about "Crusoe in England" is to say that, in it, the "I" of Borges's conceit is given another name, "Crusoe," and asked to imagine itself immersed in the details of Crusoe's life. It is important to point out that "Crusoe" stands in for this textual identity, this often otherwise unmarked "I" as much as for the historical "Bishop" who sets it in motion. The poem constitutes not so much an encrypting or encoding of autobiography—where *x* equals *y*, Crusoe equals Bishop, the island equals Brazil and so on—but rather an illustration of how autobiographically consequential moods like regret and nostalgia might be substantiated by impersonal means. "Really we had the same life," Lowell writes in "For John Berryman," "the generic one / our generation offered." Lowell's is an astonishing pronouncement since it turns on their heads the notions both of Rousseauian uniqueness (my life is mine and unlike anyone else's) and of Emersonian representativeness (my life is exemplary, and thereby universally pertinent) that underlie autobiography. The sense of having lived out a life chosen for oneself in advance, a life not essentially different from one's contemporaries, is at odds with the normative premises of autobiography that assign to each individual life its own unique signature. Lowell makes each life (within the parameters he and Berryman shared) simply interchangeable with every other life, rendering the question of uniqueness and individuality moot. The mood in Lowell's late poems is one of profound resignation, made beautiful by an obsessive awareness of temporality. Under such conditions, when one had better tell a story and any story will do, why not tell the one nearest at hand?

And yet the feeling of being no different from one's contemporaries, of having no essential or singular self, is itself an authentic premise for selfhood. For this reason one might as well tell another's story as one's own, and once that choice has been made the expressive palette becomes suddenly various and rich. "Sestina" allowed Bishop to explore the uncanniness of private memory, treating autobiography as a kind of emblem-book whose pages have fallen out, and solved, for the time being, the problem of narrative causation; but "Crusoe in England" allows her to indulge the seductions of autobiographical narrative even while distancing herself from them and to explore the structures of causal and sequential self-description. The unassailable prestige of autobiographical narrative is here deconstructed (though "deconstructed" suggests too clinical and systematic an operation) but done so in order to create the presence of a viable and specified self. If we put questions of sincerity and authenticity aside, Bishop seems to ask, if we grant all the possible objections in advance, how then might we write? If the "I" is acknowledged as its own agent, with its own career, what sort of poem will result? Naming the "I" Crusoe, calling loneliness an island, answering desire with the arrival of Friday, calling sadness Friday's absence: these are not methods exactly of representing the autobiographical self ("Bishop" or, in Borges, "Borges") but rather of freeing the rhetoric of selfhood from its slavish habitual reference upward and away from itself. "Crusoe in England" is an experiment, then, in radical contiguity. It instructs us to read autobiography as though it were myth, since it is; and it wants us to consider how much practical difference it makes, after all, what name we call ourselves by.

But of course this Crusoe is a lot like the Bishop we happen to know, and as long as even a few facts about the historical Bishop are known the poem will be read as an autobiographical myth. Undeniably, part of the pleasure the poem provides is imagining the historical Bishop behind it, holding her own life so ingeniously at an arm's length. Like the little painting in "Poem," Bishop's Crusoe myth seems to have been sitting around in an attic for a long period of time, all the while uncannily including her; it seems arced toward her and toward her discovery of it. Though it is true, as Costello writes, that the poem "draws on her wide reading, not only from Defoe but from Melville's 'The Encantadas,' Darwin's *The Voyage of the Beagle* and his autobiography, Genesis and Wordsworth" (*Questions* 208), it does so from memory, as it were, and not by any overt process of allusion. The archetypal nature of these sources is important, since at the level of archetype the personal and the communal are flush and synonymous. For this reason the two are likely to be mistaken for each other, as in the famous moment when "Crusoe" attempts to conjure a line from Wordsworth's poem "I Wandered Lonely as a Cloud":

> The books
> I'd read were full of blanks;
> The poems—well, I tried
> reciting to my iris-beds,
> "They flash upon the inward eye,
> which is the bliss . . ." The bliss of what?
> One of the first things that I did
> when I got back was look it up.
> (*Poems* 164)

According to Lloyd Schwartz, when the poem was being fact-checked by the *New Yorker*, these lines were queried (Miller 369), since it is literally impossible for Crusoe to recall (even erroneously or partially) something that hadn't yet been written and would not be written for another 150 years. Clearly these lines function as a critique of the reliance on fact of conventional autobiographical narratives, which omit so much of what is imaginatively and emotionally true in favor of a narrow and petty ledger-keeping. Beyond that, though, this act of memory is one that, by failing, requires us, requires our participation. Crusoe cannot fill in the missing word, even if he is rescued from the island, because the word will not be written for another 150 years. Bishop can but doesn't, perhaps because Crusoe himself has such trouble "finding" Wordsworth among his books 100 years too soon. This is one of Bishop's many staged inaccuracies (see also "In The Waiting Room" and "The Man-Moth"), which contribute to her effect of gawky artlessness and, thereby, sincerity. But this difficulty is especially important because, in a poem full of self-disavowals, these lines disavow the persona precisely in favor of the self and, furthermore, because it allegorizes a point of view outside of the poem that can only be ours. Our act of looking up or, better yet, recalling from memory, the missing word, makes "us" the one temporally stable site in the entire poem.

The missing word is, as we cannot help but learn, "solitude." Indeed there is a way in which the unsayability of that word governs the poem, governs, at least, our sense of its origins. Bishop's own loneliness was acute. In objecting to William Carlos Williams's inclusion of a series of anguished letters from a shunned woman in his long poem *Paterson*, Bishop wrote that "people who haven't experienced absolute loneliness for long stretches of time can never sympathize with it at all" (*Letters* 190). Bishop thought of *Robinson Crusoe* as an account not of resourcefulness but, rather, of loneliness. The sense of being alone is juxtaposed with the sense of being emphatically, repeatedly, and cruelly enumerated. The island offers only "one kind of everything":

> The island had one kind of everything:
> one tree snail, a bright violet-blue
> with a thin shell, crept over everything,

over the one variety of tree.
a sooty, scrub affair.
          (*Poems* 164)

A world that provides only single types or single examples of
types—one snail, one tree—becomes a theater of differences.
Each new phenomenon is identified by its distinguishing quality, its blue shell or its sooty bark, and the possible relations between things are vastly diminished. A snail can climb on a tree; a
sun and a man can "look" at one another, blankly, and go about
their business. Each thing exists apart from every other, and no
real syntax, no means of emphasis or subordination, ever devel-
ops. Everything in this world, like everything in the world of
Bishop's poem "Over 2,000 Illustrations and a Complete Con-
cordance," is "only connected by 'and' and 'and.'" The perils and
exhilarations of experimenting with other, more elaborate kinds
of connections are shown in two vignettes. In the first, boredom
leads to invention, intoxication, and song:

There was one kind of berry, a dark red.
I tried it, one by one, and hours apart.
Sub-acid, not bad, and no ill effects;
and so I made home-brew. I'd drink
the awful, fizzy, stinging stuff
that went straight to my head
and play my home-made flute
(I think it had the weirdest scale on earth)
and, dizzy, whoop and dance among the goats.
          (*Poems* 164)

But later the same berry—the same boredom—leads to nightmare and terror:

One day I dyed a baby goat bright red
with my red berries, just to see
something a little different.
And then his mother wouldn't recognize him.
          (*Poems* 165)

The longing for a change of color, a change of scenery, a change in the relations between things, may be the impulse governing "art," if the narrow parameters of the allegory are obeyed. But as an account of the origin of art, these vignettes are (like much of the poem) curiously overdetermined. Just as we cannot but look up or recall the word "solitude" we seem powerless to do anything but see the flute as a figure for poetry, and the twin vignettes as accounts of its risks and rewards. It is part of the poem's genius to make a profound rhetorical narrowness, a narrowness that includes our response, part of its overall design.

On the island, where there is only one of everything, there is only one possible interpretation of everything, an interpretation things have no interest in concealing or complicating (we are, after all, in paradise). The striking moments of tautology constitute the fullest expressions of this rhetorical crisis. Concerning the sun, we are told:

> The sun set in the sea; the same odd sun
> rose from the sea,
> and there was one of it and one of me.

A few lines earlier, this self-catechism:

> I often gave way to self-pity.
> "Do I deserve this? I suppose I must.
> I wouldn't be here otherwise. Was there
> a moment when I actually chose this?
> I don't remember, there could have been."
> What's wrong about self-pity, anyway?
> With my legs dangling down familiarly
> over a crater's edge, I told myself
> "Pity should begin at home." So the more
> pity I felt, the more I felt at home.
>
> (*Poems* 164)

This kind of tautological formulation, where *y* equals *x* since *x* equals *y*, is the result of being in a place where everything outside of oneself is so starkly different from oneself. Generalization, comparison, forms of abstract thought that depend on minute differences within categories are impossible here. The poem is filled with startlingly vivid descriptive passages, some of the most beautiful passages in all of Bishop, but they are curiously circumscribed or pared down, as though language itself were being rationed. Crusoe himself calls this enterprise "playing" with words; it is possible to do so, alternating between calling a mountain "Mount Despair" and "Mont D'Espoir," but more complex kinds of verbal organization seem unattainable.

The poem displays, then, along with its other imaginative insufficiencies, an idiomatic insufficiency, as though a very few expressions were being asked to perform a wide range of difficult functions. Crusoe, we must remember, is an old man in the poem, and old men in Bishop's work all tend to speak the same wide-eyed, homely idiolect. Bishop has a wonderful ear for the ways old sayings are used, by a certain class of people, to demarcate experience. This strain in her work is related to her sentimentality, her desire to test tried-and-true axioms and emblems against even shockingly new experiences. Her grandfather's advice in "Manners" hovers over Bishop's ethical system: "Be sure to remember to always / speak to everyone you meet" (*Poems* 45). It is one of Bishop's most forbidding qualities, temperamentally speaking, that she endorses such notions wholeheartedly and without irony. The doilies of "Filling Station" are another example of this desire to impersonate the manners of a world blissfully ignorant to the world of art. Crusoe is one of these figures of benign insufficiency, a kind of "old-timer" surrounded by the relics of his time and place. In "Crusoe in England" we hear about "petering out" archipelagoes and turtles that "got on my nerves"; the most common verb tense is the homey, anecdotal past imperfect ("I used to sit on the edge of the highest one"; "I'd grab his beard and look at him"); and the interjections "Oh . . ." and "Well . . ." add their hue to many otherwise simple declarative statements. This person is trying to keep a narrative going by means of old, outmoded fuel like coal or whale oil. The whole story is a kind of elegant jalopy.

Here I must pause, since it is important to ask what difference the atmosphere of staged insufficiency makes to this archetypal autobiographical narrative. It is a question the poem invites us to ask, indeed one on which a right reception of the poem depends. If we enter into a kind of reading contract when we encounter an autobiography, agreeing to put aside our skepticisms in order to be party to a sincere and honest, and even true, account of a person's life, what sort of contract does "Crusoe in England" imply? As I argued earlier, the attribution of Bishop-like characteristics to Robinson Crusoe constitutes a preemptive strike against the dismissably naive and narrow aspects of conventional autobiography. In addition, Bishop's mingled attraction to and distrust of narrative is embodied by this arm's-length self-portrayal, a portrayal of the self as immersed in the eventfulness of lived life but perhaps no more beholden to one person's set of events than another's. These are common strategies in autobiographical writing, of course; as I remark in my introduction, the genre is virtually defined by its self-conscious evasions of generic norms. It seems that sincerity always involves a kind of overt gesture of apology or self-justification as its primum mobile. But the taking-on of Crusoe is different in kind from Bishop's other uses of personae, the Gentleman of Shalott, for example, or the bizarre, nocturnal Man-Moth. (Neither of these figures constitutes a true persona, strictly speaking: both are described, in the third person, by an unnamed lyric speaker.) These figures introduce themselves to us and report on their extraordinary predicaments. Each of them is seen frozen in his moment of picturesque strangeness, and shown, in that moment, to be resourceful, imaginative, and humble even while being lonely, self-obsessed, and secretive. Each is clearly "a figure for the artist," as the saying goes, but not finally or solely so; hearing from the Man-Moth we are hearing from some frightening, poignant, and authentic place in human life that our own stubbornness kept from us. By locating her personae on the edge of their own cultures, skulking about the margins, and on the edge of ours, Bishop is making a point about the nature of identity, its slipperiness, its insolubility within cultural parameters.

But Crusoe functions very differently as a device: he is "famous" and located at the very middle of Western culture. The poem ends with a meditation on fame, which is figured as an experience of meaning as fixed and insusceptible to trope. The island was a kind of arena of cleverness, with the limits of cleverness hazy and ever-shifting; one could discover, there, too late, that it is not a good idea to dye a baby goat red, at least from the goat's point of view. The experience of remorse was possible there, as was the experience of joy, since the moral world had to be deduced from the phenomenal world. England, in contrast, is "another island / that doesn't seem like one":

> The knife there on the shelf—
> it reeked of meaning, like a crucifix.
> It lived. How many years did I
> beg it, implore it, not to break?
> I knew each nick and scratch by heart,
> the bluish blade, the broken tip,
> the lines of wood-grain on the handle . . .
> Now it won't look at me at all.
> The living soul has dribbled away.
> My eyes rest on it and pass on.
>
> (*Poems* 167)

Despite the soullessness of these objects, "the local museum's asked me to / leave everything to them." The joke here is that Crusoe *is* famous, as Bishop's attention to his story proves; the items he lists ("the flute, the knife, the shriveled shoes," trousers, a parasol) pile up in the "local museum" of the poem, relics invented by her fascination. Crusoe's exhaustion arises from Bishop's own ruthless use of him, her "exploitation" of him in the most literal sense. Fame, it seems, is the condition of being available to represent, to stand in for, anyone's suffering, as the mention of "crucifix" implies. This section of the poem allegorizes our hunger for picturesque suffering and does so by means of Bishop's own hunger. Reading these lines we are attending to Crusoe's ennui at Bishop's use of him and Bishop's own ennui at having to use him, all the while sensing the smallness, the stifling quaintness, of the stakes.

The question of who speaks, then, is of particular consequence in "Crusoe in England." The ennui and reluctance, the imaginative and idiomatic insufficiency, the sentimentality, all of these elements contribute to the sense that Crusoe and Bishop are mutually inconvenienced by this marriage of necessity called "Crusoe in England." As reluctant as Bishop is to play Crusoe, Crusoe is equally reluctant to play Bishop. The wariness and suspicion, which includes self-suspicion, of the poem, the sense of having arrived here against one's will, is of course present in the original Crusoe story. What Defoe cannot encompass, in his narrative, is the idea of recollection. The Crusoe story is told in the present tense, what might be called the subsistence-present tense. The principle of such a narrative is radically simplified, taking down as it does the events of each day and to a lesser degree the thoughts spurred by those events. The self, the journal keeper is, in such a scheme, just another passive vessel of the day's occurrences. Event X and event Y happen on the island, and they also happen, more or less simultaneously, in the narrative account of the island. Especially given the circumscribed, subsistence-level means of Crusoe's island, the device of the journal suggests a model of representation where words bear the full, direct weight and impress of experience. But autobiographical recollection posits a great distance between events and their expression and, in doing so, raises the question of organization: Why has the narrative been structured so? Which events have been given priority? Which are overshadowed, or erased entirely? To ask Crusoe, who virtually embodies the radical present tense, to recollect for us may seem almost cruel, but it is precisely that demand that we make on Bishop and indeed on ourselves when we set out to attend to or to compose an autobiographical narrative.

Since the question of who is speaking is so contestable, and therefore imaginatively vibrant, the poem's most arresting disclosure takes on special importance. This is the arrival, long deferred, of Friday:

> Just when I thought I couldn't stand it
> another minute longer, Friday came.
> (Accounts of that have everything all wrong.)
> Friday was nice.
> Friday was nice, and we were friends.
> If only he had been a woman!
> I wanted to propagate my kind,
> and so did he, I think, poor boy.
> He'd pet the baby goats sometimes,
> and race with them, or carry one around.
> —Pretty to watch; he had a pretty body.
>
> (166)

In this poem where proportionality has been explicitly at issue, where we feel a radical narrowness and scarcity governing the very means of representation, this passage on Friday calls attention to its own proportions. James Merrill writes, of these lines: "I once idiotically asked the author, on being shown this poem before publication, if there couldn't be a bit more about Friday? She rolled her eyes and threw up her hands: oh, there used to be—*lots* more! But then it seemed . . . And wasn't the poem already long enough?" (quoted in Kalstone 257) The elemental syntax, the lack of adjectival coloration, the suggestion of primal kinds of thinking (like syllogism, discussed already above), the childlike categorization ("friends"), the unmarked verb "came"— all contribute to a sense that language is slipping from a signifier too densely real and immediate to be mastered. It is Friday's proximity—in this poem of yearning, of unbearable but describable distances—that disarms description. The mere mention of his name, it seems, conjures him, and he seems to move about in the foreground of the poem.

Because Friday enters Crusoe's recollections so late, because there is proportionally little about him, and because what little there is seems so inadequate, we cannot but consider the Friday episode as a critique of disclosure, indeed of the confessional mode. (Here and elsewhere I take it for granted that the poem spurs such theoretical thinking only by being, first and foremost, genuinely moving, especially in the Friday passages.) The passage describing Friday is remarkable for its hushed restraint, a mood that carries with it important interpretive consequences. The poem's figurative decorum consists not only of Bishop's saying nothing, as Crusoe, that Crusoe couldn't say but, furthermore, of saying nothing as Crusoe that she, Bishop, couldn't say. But in the Friday vignette we find the conceit doubling itself, taking on an interpretive complexity that has the effect of isolating the "real" Elizabeth Bishop whose presence had, up to now, been obscured. The term "nice" for example, by its very innocence and naïveté, carries a sexual charge; Crusoe might say it innocently, or he might say it suggestively, depending on whether we think Friday to be a surrogate friend or surrogate wife (Defoe's text is rather famously indeterminate). Crusoe-Bishop, likewise, might say "Friday was nice" and mean it innocently (that is, without erotic content), if it is in the nature of Fridays to be surrogates for other, more libidinous relations—or is surrogacy the essence of desire? It seems clear enough what Crusoe-Crusoe means by the phrase "If only he had been a woman." But it complicates matters considerably for Crusoe-Bishop to utter such a phrase, since (from that point of view) Friday *is* a woman, that is to say, a viable object of libido. The homoerotic reimagining of *Robinson Crusoe* would tease out all of the hints and innuendoes of the original text, reemphasizing in the arrival of Friday, whom the island licenses, virtually requires, Crusoe to love. But "If only he had been a woman" is not a phrase Crusoe-Bishop would say; it could only be said by Crusoe-Crusoe or by the historical Elizabeth Bishop; the carefully tended decorum that governed the poem's central conceit runs up, suddenly, against one of its limits.

"If only he had been a woman" is one of the complexly embedded disclosures, disclosures that call into question the value and function of disclosure, which distinguish Bishop's autobiographical poems. Like the scene of Nova Scotia in "Poem," this sudden discovery of the historical self contains something evanescent, something liable to flight and disappearance, and catching it depends on situating oneself very precisely within a recalcitrant artwork. Indeed it seems that Bishop's resistance to the more transparent confessional styles—Sexton's, for example—has little to do with a notion of decorum, which would think of lyric poetry as somehow coarsened by personal disclosure. "Crusoe in England" asks us to consider the extent to which every element of a lyric poem—even, especially, the most seemingly "transparent"—is in fact staged and warns us of the perils of improper, inadequate staging for our acts of self-description.

As an autobiographical poet, Bishop offers a model for lyric that differs from Lowell's in choosing the "insignificant," even interchangeable, facts of domestic life over those of history; the perceptual over the intellectual, the displaced over the disclosed, the prismatic over the linear. Her poems therefore document the development and career of a sensibility within an autobiographical frame. That she would come closest to doing "straight" autobiography in the person of Crusoe should indicate just how imperiling the conventions of autobiography were to her. Her use of Crusoe as a mask would seem to be in some way definitive, but as we shall see in the work of Frank Bidart, the use of masks is as likely to result in emotional nakedness as it is in Bishop's exquisite reticence.

Reading Frank Bidart Pragmatically

Frank Bidart is the author of six books of poems, from *Golden State* (1971) to *Star Dust* (2005). He was born in Bakersfield, California, in 1939, the only child of parents who soon divorced. His father was a potato farmer who dreamed of being a movie cowboy; his mother considered herself a great, undiscovered beauty. The proximity to Hollywood affected Bidart as well: growing up, he dreamed of making films but turned instead, in his twenties, to writing poems; those poems have shown some stylistic attributes that may loosely be called "cinematic." After graduating from the University of California, Riverside, Bidart "became an Easterner," enrolling in the doctoral program in English at Harvard, where he was, briefly, an instructor in Reuben Brower's legendary Humanities 6 course. Brower was himself a friend and former colleague of Robert Frost; his circle at Harvard included, in addition to Bidart, a roster of critics and poets too long to enumerate here. Among them was Richard Poirier, whose own account of the course (in *Poetry and Pragmatism*) has done perhaps the most work in keeping its memory alive. A certain kind of reading practice, what Poirier has named "reading pragmatically"

(171), took shape in Brower's company. Brower himself, in a gesture evocative of the entire ambience surrounding the course, call his practice simply "reading in slow motion." In 1968 Bidart met Robert Lowell, the putative subject of his doctoral thesis; though he did not write that thesis, he became Lowell's friend, confidant, and amanuensis, advising the poet especially closely during the assembly of Lowell's last four books.

Reading Bidart closely involves reading him in several of the above contexts. In some respects he represents the far-flung consequences of Brower's pragmatics of reading: Bidart's poems are often vigorous experiments performed on preexisting texts, not all of them literary texts. Bidart often seems to be answering the fundamental pragmatist question, What can be done with this text? (The theory implicit behind that question being, Why shouldn't everything possible be done with a text?) But in other respects he represents confessionalism in its mannerist phase, after the theatrical instincts of Plath and Lowell have been acknowledged and the self, no matter how intimate, seen as essentially a performance. These two ideas are seemingly at odds: the pragmatist plays an endless number of changes on his chosen texts, limited only by his own ingenuity, while the postconfessional poet uses poetry to gain access to otherwise inaccessible "essence." But what the two ideas share is an interest in performance, in literary artifacts as both record of and script or score for performance.

Since Bidart's poems often rewrite existing texts, to encounter a Bidart poem is very much to encounter Bidart's presence—often contentious—within another, foreign, presence. The effect is peculiar, but whatever Bidart surrenders or concedes to achieve it, there is no other contemporary poet whose aesthetics seems so deliberate, even argumentative. Indeed Bidart's poems are often arguments, waged on one side or the other of a vexing question. He is a poet of "subject matter," and his subjects have at times shocked readers; his poems treat, among other things, incest, necrophilia, anonymous sex, and phone sex, prompting the charge, from some critics, of sensationalism. But although

Bidart himself insists on the importance of this transgressive "subject matter" in his poems, he is equally insistent on remaining within what Robert von Hallberg has called "the tone of the center." His subjects, despite their "sensational" trappings, tend ultimately toward those that all poets at all times have examined: the limits of the will, especially as it faces death or desire or both; the difficulty of assembling experience, especially past experience, especially one's childhood, into form; guilt and remorse; as well as poetry itself. The poet who chooses these subjects chooses the subjects that poets inevitably choose. How to justify, then, the polemical insistence on "subject matter"? Bidart explains:

> [Early in my career] ... I felt how literary, how "wanting to be like other writers"—particularly like the Modernists and post-modernists—the animating impulses behind my poems were. I said to myself (I remember this very clearly): "If what fills your attention are the great works that have been written—*Four Quartets* and *Ulysses* and "The Tower" and *Life Studies* and *Howl* ... and *The Cantos*—nothing is *left* to be done. You couldn't possibly make anything as inventive or sophisticated or complex. But if you turn from them, and what you look at is your *life*: NOTHING is figured out; NOTHING is understood. ... *Ulysses* doesn't describe your life. It doesn't teach you how to lead your life. You don't know what *love* is; or *hate*; or *birth*; or *death* or *good*; or *evil*. ... I realized that "subject matter"—confronting the dilemmas, issues, "things" with which the world had confronted me—had to be at the center of my poems if they were to have force. (*Western Night* 232)

Bidart needs subjects because his art, often so extreme in its pitch and presentation, is nevertheless essentially one of dynamic process. "I had to learn how to *use* the materials of the poem to *think*" he says, stressing the ongoingness of the process, thinking, that animates his poems. To justify such careful thought, we must sense the "issues" to be real—worth thinking about—and furthermore that the not thinking about them might well be hazardous. "All our ingenuity is lavished upon getting into danger legitimately so that we may be genuinely rescued," Robert

Frost remarks. Bidart's subjects establish some of the strangest, and thereby most difficult, and thereby "legitimate," errands ever assigned to the speaking voice.

William Pritchard ends his review of Bidart's 1977 volume *The Book of the Body* by praising Bidart's "convincing wonder" toward his subjects: "One feels he has not invented them for the sake of writing a poem" (Pritchard 64). Though this is true, no poet of our era writes poems that look more "invented"—made in order to solve a problem—than Bidart; to an unsympathetic reader, this inventiveness can feel like contrivance.

Sentence Sounds

As any visual survey of his work will reveal, Bidart is an expressionist in his poetics, making sometimes flamboyant use of the textual conventions that indicate speakerly affect—capitals and italics to mark stress and volume; combinations of two or even three forms of punctuation to chart the career of a voice as it passes through, and passes into, a sometimes labyrinthine syntax; and a sense (derived in part from Pound) of the poetic line as a material scar on the page, the sense a painter might have of her brushstrokes on the canvas. Bidart's poems simply look different from other poems, different from what he calls (in his long sequential elegy "Golden State") "mere neat poetry." He states: "What caught me about writing poems was not the fascination of using meter and rhyme—I knew somehow, however gropingly and blindly, that there must be some way to get down the motions of the voice in my head. . . . It seemed that my own speech just wasn't, as so much English has always been, basically iambic" (*Western Night* 226). The primary metrical convention by which lyric poems indicate their spokenness was, and very arguably remains, the pentameter line: individual freedom of affect (whether in Robert Frost or Robert Lowell) tends to measure itself against and within the standard five-beat iambic line. Indeed Bidart is thinking here of Frost, in this case Frost's remark that all spoken English can be mapped onto two rhythms and two only, "strict iambic and loose iambic."

But where the origin of "the speaking voice" for Frost is the overheard conversation of his neighbors "North of Boston," Bidart traces his own poetics back to "the voices in my head"—to the solitary, the antisocial. Frost's dramatic speakers (there are notable exceptions) tend to be solitary within society, isolated within conversation, and set in recognizable domestic arenas. His ur-text for this kind of speech is book 10 of *Paradise Lost*, and indeed many of his own finest poems are Miltonic dialogues between men and women. But the voices in Bidart's poems originate in consciousness (albeit in a strangely extroverted and articulate model of consciousness); their closest equivalent in drama is the soliloquy or, in opera, the aria. His speakers tend to be literally (and often newly) isolated, left suddenly alone by the death of a parent or a lover, by the end of a year of their life or by the century's end, and further isolated by the extremity of their emotional or intellectual—their philosophical—despair. Both Bidart and Frost cast lyric, at least in part, as the translation of an antecedent spoken (or heard-as-spoken) voice into written, and thereby infinitely repeatable, form; both would likely agree with Helen Vendler's definition of lyric as a "score for the voice of the reader" (*Sonnets* 12). Both imagine lyric as a form of writing emerging from, before disappearing back into, speech. But the irremediable solitude implicit in Frost becomes the premise in Bidart, most of whose speakers speak to themselves, or to the dead, or from beyond the grave, or from a past largely beyond imaginative retrieval; there are few dialogues in his poems, few interlocutors to encourage or check the course of self-revelatory speech.

"Actuality and intimacy are the greatest aim an artist can have," Frost writes. "The sense of intimacy gives the thrill of sincerity" (664). But Bidart's notion of what "actuality" *sounds* like, of precisely which acoustic arrangements or conditions might best convey the sensation of selfhood (and of "sincerity") differs markedly from Frost's. Frost's theory of "sentence sounds" is based on the principle of overheard dialogue, where the "sound of sense" arises from the sounds men and women make when they need to *make* sense:

> The best place to get the abstract sound of sense is from voices behind a door that cuts off the words. Ask yourself how these sentences would sound without the words in which they are embodied:
>
> You mean to tell me you can't read?
> I said no such thing.
> Well read then.
> You're not my teacher.
>
> (665)

Frost's sense of "actuality" depends on an originary absence (or perhaps invisibility) of art; however profound Frost is on the topic of imaginative making, however allegorically we read poems that are purportedly about mowing or stone-boats or home burial, not one of his speakers acknowledges the fact of the frame, even in conforming to the representational limits of the frame. Frost's speakers remain "natural," speaking to us from what the poet calls "the hard everyday world of the street, business, trades, work in summer." Their immersion in tasks beyond the reach of (yet analogous to) literary writing ensures that none of Frost's speakers will speak beyond themselves, that their speech tones will be compelled by necessity rather than chosen by fancy. (Such speakerly naïveté is also necessary for Frost's allegory; we can read "The Death of the Hired Man" as, in part, an allegory of poetic composition precisely because its participants cannot.) The need of the worker (or the quarreling lover) to eliminate superfluous and peripheral sense data from consciousness (what William James calls "the narrowing of consciousness") is a figure for the poet's own act of murderous exclusion, his interest in and only in "material." Similarly, the speech of "work" is likely to carry heightened stakes for the communication of sense and is, therefore, likely to be more richly attentive to its own sounds.

Where Frost's "technical" interest is in dialogue, in the tones people resort to in making sense to one another, Bidart's own ear was formed on a different sort of speech: the "delivered" or "performed" monologue, the speech whose premise is in part its own acknowledgment of artifice and style. Frost's project (an Emersonian one) is to return language back to its original condition of "poetic" effect, and he does so both by imitating forms of candor—the language of work, the language of argument—and by casting his poems as "overheard." But where Emerson elegizes a world where "every word was a poem," Frost imagines a world of speech even before the dawn of words, where words, like Adam's fig leaf, become the visible sign of our corruption. It would be absurd to say that Frost isn't concerned with diction, because of course he is; but equally it is important to acknowledge how often he conveys the sensation of strangeness and of poetic "newness" by eliminating precisely those units of diction—substantives, strong verbs, adjectives—that conventionally bear a sentence's meaning. (The first line of his late poem "Directive" is a fine example: "Back out of all this now too much for us.")

Unlike Frost, Bidart tends to think of the voices prior to and subject to his poetics as complexly mediated by self-conscious performance. In his prose poem "Borges and I," Bidart argues that there is properly no self, for an artist, separate from or antecedent to "the self who makes [art]." He describes himself in the third person listening, as a child, to a record of Olivier performing Hamlet's advice to the players: "He felt terror at the prospect of becoming again and again the person who could find or see or make no mirror, for even Olivier, trying to trap the beast who had killed his father, when he suavely told Frank as Frank listened to the phonograph long afternoons lying on the bed as a kid, when Olivier told him what art must be, even Olivier insisted that art is a mirror held up by an artist who himself needs to see something, held up before a nature that recoils before it" (*Desire* 11). It is difficult, it is made difficult, to sort among the many levels and stages of address in this scene: in the arena called *Hamlet*, Hamlet is advising the players about how to "speak the speech"

naturally—which precisely means without the usual stage conventions that indicate "naturalness"; but he is doing so for his own
submerged, "artificial" reason, "to trap the beast who had killed his
father"; and furthermore doing so (from our point of view) manifestly as a character in a play. The "speak the speech" speech is
therefore, even in Shakespeare's conception—even, that is, in its
simplest form—an incooperatively complex exemplum of speech,
a palimpsest of motives and styles, about as far from a "sincere"
speech act (whatever that might be) as possible. To add another
level of complexity, though, it is a particular performance of the
speech—Olivier's—that Bidart remembers; but that ephemeral
performance is the recorded one, the one preserved for infinite
repetition. In that site of instruction, "Frank Bidart's bedroom,"
it is "Olivier" who speaks Hamlet's speech and Bidart who listens;
putting Bidart, therefore, in the duped and manipulated position
of the players. But of course it is Bidart who addresses us in the
arena called "reader reading Frank Bidart"; and as any reader of
Bidart knows, "trapping the beast who had killed his father" (as
well as the beast who was his father) is among this poet's central
obsessions. Bidart's own "recording device" is the poem in our
hands; as such it (like the record spinning on the record player in
Bakersfield, California, in the fifties) records only one of several
"takes" and in doing so renders that take the real, the "actual" one.

Bidart's fundamental practice, then, is to treat the composition
of voice like transcription, like a "taking down" of speech that
precedes his own; such "taking down," though, cannot embody
the fullness of speech by merely recording speech; the passage
of speech into writing involves an exorbitant exchange rate, and
that exchange rate must be acknowledged and compensated for
by linguistic means. Poirier has described the "feeling" induced
by Reuben Brower's teaching "that the human presence in any
gathering of words was always elusive, existing as it did in the
very tentative, sometimes self-doubting plays of sound" (Poirier
171). That "human presence," Brower would say, depends on the
creation of an acoustics within which the quiet sound of a voice

making discoveries about itself becomes audible. Bidart, for his part, often writes the way Brower read—that is, with an ear to the submerged "human presence" in existing texts. This fact is especially important in understanding Bidart's frequent use of existing writing—existing "voice"—to offset and underscore his own voice. In an interview Bidart has described his attempts, for an early poem, to rewrite a sentence of Dr. Johnson, "The mind can only rest on the stability of truth": "As I heard this sentence, it had a weight and grimness, a large finality it just didn't have when I first typed it. In the attempt to *make* the sentence look the way I heard it, I typed the words hundreds of different ways, with different punctuation and line breaks, for weeks" (*Western Night* 224). Bidart eventually gives up, he says; but this sort of strenuous rewriting remains an essential element of his poetics. Since voice exists in every case prior to writing, an existing text may not look the way it sounds—making the rewriting of texts an especially rich arena for the performance of individual affect. The tonal and inflectional identity we call "Frank Bidart" has emerged "through" the diaries of Nijinsky, through Binswanger's case study of Ellen West, through Ovid; Bidart has even done a demotic rewriting of the opening of the book of Genesis.

People: "Ellen West"

Pragmatic experimentation on texts would on its own qualify as a very arid and academic purpose for writing lyric poems. But the problem of writing presence into texts—a problem I describe above in terms of the translation of existing but insufficiently "voiced" texts into life (whether a sentence from Dr. Johnson or Rossetti's Dante) takes on an ethical dimension for Bidart. The writing of a poem can seem like an act of recovery or intervention for the poet, and this sensation of the ethical can be passed along, like any other effect, as part of the reader's experience of a poem. Frost, for example, called his *North of Boston* a "book of people," thereby suggesting that we hear the book as spoken by people—not, that is, by Frost—and read it with the kind of sympathy we might grant to an real person actually confiding in us.

There is no book of Bidart's that could not share Frost's description of *North of Boston*. His work is profoundly an affair of people, but Bidart's people tend to be recovered not from "life" (where, presumably, they were "lost" in rural kitchens and orchards, out of the earshot of "Boston") but rather from texts. The closer Bidart gets to the self, the more he must "cast" that self as a character. The final section of Bidart's most explicitly autobiographical poem, "Golden State," opens with an explanation of such "dramatic" strategies of self-presentation:

> When I began this poem,
> > to see myself
> as a piece of history, having a past
> which shapes, and informs, and thus inevitably
> limits—
> > at first this seemed sufficient, the beginning of
> freedom . . .
> > The way to approach freedom
> was to acknowledge necessity:—
> I sensed I had to become not merely
> a speaker, the "eye," but a character . . .
> > > (*Western Night* 162)

The self (the "speaker") exists only within the absurdity of form—an absurdity lessened only by "acknowledging" that necessary assumption of form. This idea shapes Bidart's poetics; but it is a poetics that cannot help but see (and "acknowledge") its own metaphysical dimensions. In Bidart's metaphysics the mind needs, and yet despises, the body; love exists but only as it is manifested in the bodies of lovers whose bodies are mortal. For the self to pass into art it must itself assume form, one form or another; the necessity of form is the origin of style. But style is always only a temporary solution to a permanent problem, the problem of "dressing" the inner life in a manner that will make it imaginatively, intellectually, and culturally communicable. Once the "power" of a poem is embodied in "form" (to use Emerson's terms) it is defined by all the chauvinisms native to that form; and no matter how durable that form, it must eventually take its place in the history of durable forms. Or as Bidart says (in "Happy Birthday") of some early twentieth-century bicycle racers whose trading-card pictures he discovers: "Terrible to dress in the style / Of a period that must end" (*Western Night* 94).

Bidart's interest in choosing noncanonical texts owes a debt to Brower: in "Hum 6" Brower read art (Poirier mentions *Portrait of the Artist as a Young Man* and *The Adventures of Huckleberry Finn*) beside other documents—manuals, course books, anonymous diaries—more "found" than "made." Bidart, for his part, has rewritten Dante, Ovid, and Genesis but also the songs of Al Green, personal letters, and the memoirs of Hector Berlioz. Underlying this ambition is a desire like Brower's to "do things" with texts—not, that is, to treat them as loci of stable and portable "meaning" but rather as sites for the performance—fluid, self-revising—of human presence. Great poems are more likely, on average, to have been already fully voiced by their authors; other, less attentively shaped documents might provide a different kind of lesson in the retrieval of voice, a different kind of reading lesson.

Noncanonical texts are more likely, as well, to carry the pathos of lost or neglected things; and where the text itself concerns a kind of loss, is itself the record of a loss, the pathos is thereby compounded. This is the case with Bidart's long poem "Ellen West," an adaptation of one of the case histories of the psychoanalyst Ludwig Binswanger. The poem is both a transfiguration of Binswanger's prose and a searching account of how that text, how any text, could be transfigured; and since the poem records the story of a woman who herself could not be kept alive, it is at every level an attempt to retrieve human presence from all the institutions that muffle and suppress it—including the institution called "art" that deems such documents beneath or outside of its concern. In assuming a dramatic speaker Bidart also assumes a preexisting verbal form; the poem inhabits a bounded consciousness, Ellen West's, at the same time as it adapts a narrative document, Binswanger's. "Ellen West" additionally is a poem about the attempt to perfect the physical body (West is an anorexic) according to the dictates of the spirit. The anorexic seeks an accurate "representation" of spirit, a sign that will refer to spirit with as little slippage as possible; the dream of the anorexic is for sign (body) and referent (spirit) to become indistinguishable from one another. But in doing so, as Louise Glück points out, the very sign the anorexic trusts (the body) decays and eventually dies precisely because of such an investment of trust.

"Ellen West" describes a widening schism between the mandates of West's psyche—her "true self"—and those of her doctors. West introduces herself as an allegory of her own appetites:

> I love sweets,—
> > heaven
> would be dying on a bed of vanilla ice cream . . .
>
> But my true self
> is thin, all profile
>
> and effortless gestures, the sort of blond
> elegant girl whose
> > > body is the image of her soul.
>
> —My doctors tell me I must give up
> this ideal;
> > but I
> WILL NOT . . . cannot.
>
> Only to my husband I'm not simply a "case."
>
> But he is a fool. He married
> meat, and thought it was a wife.
> > > > (*Western Night* 109)

The opinions of the world enter, here, in secondary position ("My doctors tell me . . ." "He . . . thought [I] was a wife"), as conditions contrary to fact. As the poem unfolds it will be clear that the only real conversation is between "self" and "true self"; the husband never speaks, and the doctor's opinions, while meant to "refer" to Ellen's case, merely punctuate it, in the manner of a Sophoclean chorus. As in Sophocles, this chorus can express merely the grammar, so to speak, of the unfolding sentence, its underlying rules and principles; it can't interfere with the semantic content of the play as the play unfolds. This fact is of course bitterly ironic, since it is precisely the aspiration of the diagnosis to name and thereby diminish Ellen West's "condition." These diagnostic opinions are separated from the body of the poem by asterisks, and rendered in flat, "artless" prose, all the more wrenching when we realize that *their* distance from Ellen West suggests our own, the distance of any reader from any text, the distance of this essay from the poem called "Ellen West." (These sections employ an impoverished "descriptive" language—"tortured" vomiting, "violent" diarrhea, "thinned down to a skeleton"—that reinforces this sense of hideous spectatorship.)

Ellen West is herself a poet, as her doctors tell us; and so the question of poetic style and its relation to embodiment is one that exists within the poem's own parameters. The log for "January 21" reads: "Has been reading *Faust* again. In her diary, writes that art is the 'mutual permeation' of the 'world of the body' and the 'world of the spirit.' Says that her own poems are 'hospital poems . . . weak—without skill or perseverance; only managing to beat their wings softly'" (*Western Night* 113). Ellen West's dismissal of her poems ("hospital poems") carries none of the spite or self-hatred of her dismissal of her own body; and in the long passage that follows we learn that the model for West's own kind of self-perfection is not the art of the writer, who creates a body-not-his-own that lives on after and apart from him, but rather that of the performer, whose art and body are contiguous and inseparable. The performer must, in making of his body the medium of his art, account and compensate for the limitations of the body. Furthermore, in the very act of writing, a writer creates the record of the act of writing; but no such record is made, for a singer, by the very act of singing.

Helen Vendler has called Bidart's monologues "written arias for solo voice" (*Part* 123), an insight that captures their elaborate staging as well as their tonal pitch. This "interpenetration" of body and voice, artist and artifact, emerges as the topic of West's long digression on the singer Maria Callas.

> Callas is my favorite singer, but I've only
> seen her once—;
>
> I've never forgotten that night . . .
>
> —It was in *Tosca*, she had long before
> lost weight, her voice
> had been, for years,
>   deteriorating, half itself . . .
> When her career began, of course, she was fat,
>
> enormous—; in the early photographs,
> sometimes I almost don't recognize her . . .
>
> The voice too then was enormous—
>
> healthy; robust; subtle; but capable of
> crude effects, even vulgar,
>   almost out of
> high spirits, too much health.
>   (*Western Night* 113–14)

As Callas's body changes (she loses sixty pounds in four months) her voice changes; and as her voice changes, West thinks, her art must respond to a new, more dire imperative: to represent not "the song" (or, in an opera, the "character") but rather her "soul," a soul that is manifested by her newly thinned body:

> —The gossip in Milan was that Callas
> had swallowed a tapeworm.
>
> But of course she hadn't.
>
>   The *tapeworm*
>
> was her *soul*.
>   (*Western Night* 115)

"Her soul, uncompromising, / insatiable / must have loved eating the flesh from her bones"—the "soul" thins Callas to her new form just as a sculptor trims excess marble from a sculpture, revealing "this extraordinary / mercurial; fragile; masterly creature":

> —But irresistibly, nothing
> *stopped* there; the huge voice
>
> also began to change. at first, it simply diminished
> in volume, in size,
>   then the top notes became
> shrill, unreliable—at last,
> usually not there at all . . .
>
> —No one knows *why*. Perhaps her mind,
> ravenous, still insatiable, sensed
>
> that to struggle with the *shreds* of a voice
>
> must make her artistry subtler, more refined,
> more capable of expressing humiliation,
> rage, betrayal . . .
>
> —Perhaps the opposite. Perhaps her spirit
> loathed the unending struggle
>
> to *embody* itself, to *manifest* itself, on a stage whose
> mechanics, and suffocating customs,
> seemed expressly designed to annihilate spirit.
>   (*Western Night* 115)

In the course of performance, then, Callas must meet and incorporate her own expressive limits; must account for (which is to say, make beautiful) the "shrillness" and "unreliability" of her notes. So the performance of song turns into a performance of self; the subtle adjustments by which Callas makes the contours of song available to her is a model for the way an individual human life creates itself within the "givens" of generalized experience and fate. West describes how, in watching

Tosca she, West, suddenly "felt like I was watching / autobiography":

> —I know that in *Tosca*, in the second act,
> when, humiliated, hounded by Scarpia,
> she sang *Vissi d'arte*
> > —"I lived for art"—
>
> and in torment, bewilderment, at the end she asks,
> with a voice reaching
> > harrowingly for the notes,
>
> "Art has *repaid* me LIKE THIS?"
> > (*Western Night* 116)

Callas's ability to "be Callas" while playing in *Tosca* (like Olivier's inexorable "Olivier"-ness even, especially when playing the most famous role in Western drama) figures Ellen West's own wish to "be Ellen West" within a role, perhaps "girl" or "wife"; the sad difference, invisible of course to Ellen West, is that Callas adapts her voice to the necessities of her body, not vice versa. The body dies at the very moment the dictates of voice are at last obeyed; we know this because its inverse—that is, that voice itself "dies" of its perfect embodiment—is true in the case of Callas, as West concludes:

> —I wonder what she feels, now,
> listening to her recordings.
>
> For they have already, within a few years,
> begun to date . . .
>
> Whatever they express
> they express through the style of a decade
> and a half—;
> > a style *she* helped create . . .
>
> —She must know that now
> she probably would *not* do a trill in
> *exactly* that way,—
> > that the whole sound, atmosphere,

dramaturgy of her recordings

have just slightly become those of the past . . .

—Is it bitter? Does her soul
tell her

that she was an *idiot* ever to think
anything
material wholly could satisfy?
—Perhaps it says: *The only way*
to escape
the History of Styles

is not to have a body.

(Western Night 116)

In the following section West interprets the parable of Callas and *Tosca*, asking whether "without a body" anyone can "*know* himself at all" and deciding, in a fatal leap of logic, that the only route to "spirit" is not the *via negativa* of starvation but, rather, the affirmative act of suicide (as we later learn) by poison:

This *I* is anterior

to name; gender; action;
       fashion;
          MATTER ITSELF,—

. . . trying to stop my hunger with FOOD
is like trying to appease thirst

          with ink.

(Western Night 117–18)

That "ink" prefigures the suicide note that closes the poem; where the poem had been, up to that final section, form-within-form (Bidart's within Binswanger's) it ends as form-within-form-within-form (Bidart's within Binswanger's within West's). The final irony is West's desire to pass out of the body; and yet the manifest presence of form (not just a letter but a suicide letter, among the most convention bound of all varieties of letters) provides the stage for Ellen West's last, and most intimate, performance of voice. The addressee is the friend to whom she had grown close during her stay in the hospital:

> Dearest,—I remember how
> at eighteen,
>   on hikes with friends, when
> they rested, sitting down to joke or talk,
>
> I circled
> around them, afraid to hike ahead alone,
> yet afraid to rest
> when I was not yet truly thin.
>
> You and, yes, my husband,—
> you and he
>
> have by degrees drawn me within the circle;
> forced me to sit down at last on the ground.
>
> I am grateful.
>
> But something in me *refuses* it.
>   (*Western Night* 121)

In "trying to kill this refuser" West only intensifies the "ideal" of thinness; every concession or compromise heightens the desire to pass outside the world of social contingency where compromise is the rule. The "circle" represents not merely "society" but the idea of boundedness, of embodiedness; when West "enters" the circle her crusading desire, which had become synonymous with life, must be surrendered, and she must end her life.

The first ambition of "Ellen West" is to be moving, which is to say "actual" and "intimate" (to use Frost's terms); this ambition seems simple enough—what work of art doesn't aspire to be moving?—until we realize two things: first, that actuality and intimacy in any verbal artifact will depend on effects of language, and language, especially literary language, is a medium that by nature resists such effects; and second, that this representational paradox is in large part the explicit subject of the poem. The capacity of Ellen West for such sophisticated self-interpretation is a strange and new way for a work of art to "act natural"; in another poet's hands we might sense the "actuality" of Ellen West to be diminished by her ability to read herself as a parable, not, as in "Ellen West," heightened by precisely that skill. Bidart's speakers tend to be artists for just this reason, namely, that only to an artist is the nature of existence explicitly bound up with acts of artifactual embodiment. There is no moment in "Ellen West," then, where West is purely either a parable or an "actual" woman, because it is the very condition of West to see herself in metaphorical terms. When I speak, then, of the "theoretical" implications of the poem, I do not mean to isolate them from its "human" implications (the very fact that I can only render the distinction in quotation marks, as a purported distinction, supports my point). Profoundly, all the "ideas" in "Ellen West" have bodies attached to them, and vice versa.

The poem, then, can be read as an analysis of its own operations and of Bidart's operations in general. The presence of voice—Poirier's "human presence"—is in Bidart's practice always brought into being by work (and often quite strenuous-seeming work) done on existing linguistic structures. The self doesn't "feel" something and in turn "express" it; rather, the self encounters a verbal artifact, a "body" that resembles it enough to attract its attention but resists it enough to necessitate work. Brower's old imperative—"Let's see what they can *do* with it"—is somewhere behind this way of addressing texts. "Voice"—Ellen West's and Frank Bidart's—takes on human presence at the moment it meets and incorporates limitation. West is to her own body as Bidart is to his poem's; his straining lineation and syntax imitate West's (and Callas's) desire to separate voice from body. Eventually, though, as both West and Bidart know, the two, body and voice, must be understood as contiguous.

Pragmatic Confessions: "The Second Hour of the Night"

By naming an early poem "confessional" and by staging personal revelation so elaborately, Bidart's career is meant to historicize confessionalism, a radical act. That candor and disclosure are themselves historically conditioned gestures, that there is no poetic style outside of and exempt from the history of styles: this remains a bold assertion, and one that Bidart's poems keep making in new and invigorating ways. The limits of the confessional lyric were reached faster perhaps than those of any comparable lyric "school" or movement, in part because of Robert Lowell's powerful disavowals of his own technique. Charles Altieri memorably describes those limits, crediting Jonathan Holden for devising a "useful strategy for discovering basic assumptions of a dominant mode that no empirical survey is likely to elicit":

> We can locate influential shared assumptions by asking . . . a poetry workshop to suggest revisions for a poem written in the past. A typical contemporary litany is easy to produce: Craft must be made unobtrusive so that the work appears spoken in a natural voice; there must be a sense of urgency and immediacy to this "affected naturalness" so as to make it appear that one is reexperiencing the original event; there must be a "studied artlessness" that gives a sense of spontaneous personal sincerity; and there must be a strong movement toward emphatic closure, a movement carried on primarily by the poet's manipulation of narrative structure. (Altieri 10)

It is hard to imagine any style that, measured by this method, would be defensible. And the force of Altieri's argument is blunted by the fact that, in the fifteen years or so since his book appeared, the kind of normative postconfessional poem he describes has all but vanished, replaced by an equally dull, though more theoretically alert, sort of poem. Nevertheless Altieri's is an accurate description of the consensus poem of the 1970s and early 1980s, the sort of poem Bidart deliberately did not and would not write.

This final section, then, will attempt to account for the difference between Bidart's poems in propria persona and those of his contemporaries, a difference that is surprising given the coincidences I have just described. I will treat his long elegy for Joe Brainard, "The Second Hour of the Night"—as "voiced" and "urgent" and immediate and narrative and sincere a poem as one is likely to find and, yet, not a poem Altieri, in describing postconfessionalism, could have predicted.

"The Second Hour of the Night" was published in 1997's *Desire*. It is part of a larger structure still coming into being: there are, at least in conception, to be twelve "hours" of the night, twelve poems, each one corresponding to one of the twelve hours through which the sun must pass in the Egyptian Book of the Dead. Bidart has so far written three. The poem is as stylistically varied internally as any Bidart has written, opening and closing with dreamlike elegiac lyrics and passing, in between, through an excerpt from the memoirs of Hector Berlioz and a long retelling of Ovid's tale of Cinyras and Myrrha. These stories function as exempla of different lengths of how the workings of desire frame the workings of will. The poem's theme (acknowledged, typically, within the poem itself) is "fate embedded in the lineaments of desire"—the notion that what the Greeks called fate we might call, instead desire and that the same lavish punishments that awaited the Greeks who attempted to counteract or resist fate await us if we resist desire. In Bidart, the terms "fate" and "desire" are braided together, as they were for the Greeks; but for us fate is a debased currency, meaning nothing more than "what ends up happening." The poem, then, explores not only the inextricable nature but also the synonymous nature of fate and desire.

It is impossible to treat all of the aspects of "The Second Hour of the Night" here; I wish to focus on one, namely, the means of establishing the presence (Poirier's "human presence") of Bidart within the dense textual fabric of the poem that all but hides him. Bidart's personae have frequently been writers or thwarted writers (Nijinsky, West); but the writer that the unnamed speaker of "The Second Hour" resembles most is Bidart himself. That said, "The Second Hour" introduces its autobiographical ground-note late, and with little flourish—opening, as it does, with a hallucinatory overture or credits sequence:

On such a night
            after the countless

    assemblies, countless solemnities, the infinitely varied
    voyagings in storm and in calm observing the differences

among those who are born, who live together, and die,

*

On such a night

at that hour when

slow bodies like automatons begin again to move down

into the earth beneath the houses in which they
live bearing the bodies they desired and killed and now

bury in the narrow crawl spaces and unbreathing abrupt
descents and stacked leveled spaces these used

bodies make them dig and open out and hollow for new
veins whose ore could have said *I have been loved* but whose

voice has been rendered silent by the slow bodies whose descent
into earth is as fixed as the skeletons buried within them

*

On such a night

at that hour in the temple of

delight, when appetite
feeds on itself,—

(*Desire* 27–28)

The poem establishes the existing order of an existing hour, and
a "kind of night" within all the possible nights—what M. M.
Bakhtin calls a "chronotope." Bidart's poem is therefore a kind of
travelogue; and one of the sights this hour presents is the passage
that immediately follows, where Bidart in propria persona recalls
from the memoirs of Hector Berlioz, the moment when the
composer contemplates his wife's dead body:

On such a night, perhaps, Berlioz wrote those pages

in his autobiography which I first read when my mother
was dying, and which to me now inextricably
call up

not only her death but her life:—

"A sheet already covered her. I drew it back.

Her portrait, painted in the days of
her splendor,

       hung beside the bed—

I will not attempt to describe the grief that possessed me.

                         (*Desire* 28)

This long corridor of time—with Bidart at one end "recollecting" and the portrait of Berlioz's wife ("painted in the days of her splendor") at the other—passes through many rooms: first the "now" of the poem, then the "first time" Bidart reads Berlioz's words, then the night ("on such a night") when Berlioz himself wrote those words, and further back still, the scene by the deathbed and, finally, the portrait. Both the nearest thing to us (the poem itself) and the farthest (the portrait) are artworks, suggesting (as the poem does at many other points) that all sites of origin and consummation are themselves, like the media through which they pass, made-up things. (It also reminds us that the poem is an elegy for a painter, while further suggesting the great and complex distance between any elegy and its subject.)

The first occurrence of the "I," then, is both baldly autobiographical—as the "real" Bidart (explicitly a reader and a writer) remembers his "real" mother's death—and insistently narrative; and yet our readerly craving for more of the Bidart story is thwarted by our sudden and unexpected immersion in Berlioz's story. The "inextricability" of the two stories makes the one, Berlioz's, a substitute for the other, Bidart's. Bidart cannot, as Berlioz does, "write autobiography" since (unlike Berlioz) he must in doing so pass through and pass into his own medium, language. The one kind of autobiography, then (memoir), must be made, translated, into the other; Bidart does this by scoring Berlioz for his own, Bidart's, voice. When Berlioz describes the death of his wife, the actress Henriette-Constance Smithson, he does so "as" Bidart, just as Bidart "writes autobiography" as Berlioz. Since all the words are (at least according to the poem's premise) Berlioz's, their affective content depends on our sensing

Bidart's presence behind them, a presence established by subtleties of pacing, timing, and linear and prosodic organization:

> At eight in the evening the day of her death
> as I struggled across Paris to notify
> the Protestant minister required for the ceremony,
> the cab in which I rode, *vehicle*
> *conceived in Hell*, made a detour and
>
> took me past the Odeon:—
>
> it was brightly lit for a play then much in vogue.
>
> There, twenty-six years before, I discovered
> Shakespeare and Miss Smithson at the same moment.
>
> *Hamlet*. Ophelia. There
> I saw Juliet for the first and last time.
>
> Within the darkness of that arcade on many
> winter nights I feverishly
> paced or watched frozen in despair.
>
> Through that door I saw her enter
> for a rehearsal of *Othello*.
>
> She was unaware of the existence of
> the pale disheveled youth with
> haunted eyes staring after her—
>
> *There I asked the gods to allow her*
> *future to rest in my hands.*
>
> If anyone should ask you, Ophelia, whether the unknown
> youth without reputation or position
> leaning back within the darkness of a pillar
>
> will one day become your
> husband and prepare your last journey—
>
> with your great inspired eyes
> answer, *"He is a harbinger of woe."*
>
> (*Desire* 29)

The discovery of "Shakespeare and Miss Smithson at the same moment" suggests our own discovery of Berlioz-in-Bidart and Bidart-in-Berlioz, personality emerging most movingly precisely where, for a moment, it strains to hide itself. Bidart's "autobiography" here remains conjectural, just out of focus: something about a mother and son, something about a lover and a beloved. Though we are instructed to read the Berlioz as "calling up" a story about Frank Bidart, this conjuring must not be so explicit as to make the Berlioz story vanish. Berlioz's own primary unit of expression, the prose sentence, must still be visible and coherent within Bidart's insistent lineation; prose's own means of emphasis (italics, punctuation, the alternation of short and long sentences) must be preserved and balanced against the special resources of poetry. Poetry can put a spatial divide between the word "feverishly" and the word "paced"—preserving the immediacy and artlessness of Berlioz (whose authenticity rides on his being not-a-writer) within the linguistic self-consciousness of Bidart (who, as a writer, needs to acknowledge the cliché as a cliché in order to keep our faith.)

The logic of autobiography would dictate that, having proposed the Berlioz story as a parable of selfhood, the next section of the poem interpret that parable. Instead we get (after a short, hypnotic précis of what is to follow) a twenty-five-page retelling of the Ovidian tale of Cinyras and Myrrha, a tale that in Ovid is about a quarter as long. In the *Metamorphoses* book 10, Myrrha, daughter of Cinyras the King of Cyprus, falls in love with her father and tricks him into having sex. The overt self-reference that framed the Berlioz tale is all but gone from the tale of Cinyras and Myrrha; there is no "I" in all of the twenty-five pages. It would be impossible in this short a space to convey all of the aspects of Bidart's retelling of this Ovidian tale, so I will limit my focus to one: namely, the establishment of authorial "presence" in this seemingly most impersonal of stories. This presence is less immediately detectable in "The Second Hour of the Night" than in any other of Bidart's major poems, the marks of "personality" more subdued; even his characteristic means of emphasis (capitals, italics, exaggerated spacing) are deliberately hushed. The presentation of material is everywhere less overtly dramatic, less explicitly "voiced." And yet arguably the stakes for establishing presence and vocal urgency are greater here than ever; Bidart has never before "retold" a tale already so familiar, so much an existing part of the culture, and never at such length.

In expanding the Ovidian narrative, Bidart makes narrativity both the subject of his "Cinyras and Myrrha" and its richest metaphor; it is both a story about telling stories and a story about what stories, in being told, accomplish. It is at moments of intense narrativity, when the pace of action and disclosure is being manifestly and self-consciously regulated, that voice emerges most vividly. This is the principle, too, of the entire poem; but it is perhaps best heard in moments where the delay implicit in narrative and the delay implicit in desire coincide. In the following passage, Myrrha remembers a moment when her father, frustrated at her refusal to choose among her many suitors, lists them to her and asks her what sort of man, if any at all, she is looking for. In the Humphries translation of Ovid, the vignette occupies only ten or so lines:

> He named them over to her, asked her questions,
> Which one of them she would most prefer as husband.
> She made no answer, only stared, and seemed
> Confused in mind, and wept, and Cinyras
> Thought this was natural for a girl, and, kindly,
> Bade her not weep, and dried her cheeks, and kissed her.
> That made her happy. So—*what kind of husband?*
> "A man like you" she said. He praised her answer
> Not knowing what it really meant.
>
> (245)

In Bidart, the moment is slowed down, played over and over again, listened to with pained but fascinated concentration. A refrain of advance and retreat without forward progress runs

through this section of the poem, characterizing both the action
of the poem and its narrative strategy:

> *four steps forward then*
> *one back, then three*
> *back, then four forward.*

The refrain punctuates a narrative whose sympathies are almost
wholly, in this scene anyway, with Myrrha:

> Today when Myrrha's father reminded her that
> on this date eighteen
> years earlier her mother announced that he
> was the man whom she would in one month
>
> marry,—
>
> and then, in exasperation, asked what Myrrha
> *wanted* in a husband, unsupplied by the young men cluttering his
> court in pursuit of her hand and his throne,—
> after she, smiling, replied, "You,"
>
> blushing, he turned
> away, pleased.

A few lines later Bidart retells the scene widening the circle as
he retraces it:

> today her father, not ten feet from where
> once, as a child, she had in
> glee leapt upon him surrounded by
> soldiers and he, then, pretending to be overwhelmed
> by a superior force fell backwards with
> her body clasped in his arms as they rolled
> body over body down the long slope
> laughing and that peculiar sensation of his weight
> full upon her and then
> not, then full upon her, then not,—
> until at the bottom for a half-
> second his full weight rested upon her, then not,—

> ... not ten feet from where what
> never had been repeated except within
> her today after reminding her that today her mother
>
> exactly at her age chose him,—
>
> after she had answered his question
> with, "You,"
>
> blushing, he turned
> away, pleased.
>
> (*Desire* 40–41)

The principle of this kind of narration is repetition and variation, verse and refrain; but as with any such manifestly artful organization of data, the experience of reading this passage is one of almost excruciating delay, a slowing down to, and beyond, the constituent parts "father," "daughter," "marriage," and their synonyms. This hesitation mimics Myrrha's own hesitation in pursuing her father, but such hesitation heightens desire and is, therefore, a form of action. "What is sweet about delay is that / What emerges in spite of it is revealed as inevitable." It is inevitable that Myrrha will be punished, as she is when she is transformed into the myrrh tree that bears her name, and it is just as inevitable that the child born of her "bitter" union with her father will be the blessed Adonis. (As it is, in turn, inevitable that Adonis's beauty will provoke the jealousy of Venus.) This is Myrrha's faith, of course: if love outlasts delay it must therefore be authentic. What she does not see is what we are made to see: that the "delay" between a bitter event and its sweet outcome may last several lifetimes. The Cinyras and Myrrha story closes with a short, haunting Eliotic warning to the reader, presumably consoled that his own erotic life presents fewer obstacles than Myrrha's:

> *O you who looking within the mirror discover in*
> *gratitude how common, how lawful your desire*
>
> *before the mirror*

> *anoint your body with myrrh*
> *precious   bitter resin.*
>   (*Desire* 58)

There are lawful and unlawful ways to transgress, Bidart thinks; but the nature of desire, in being bound up with transgression, always inevitably points to the unlawful transgression.

>>><<<

"Autobiography" in Bidart has always meant the career and ultimately the fate of a voice—candid, fastidious, guilty—unmistakably his. Only incidentally has that voice told us things about the man, Frank Bidart, who created it. The strange thing about "The Second Hour of the Night," though, is that the voice we've grown accustomed to over the career is here muffled, and a new voice emerges in its place. Bidart is profoundly the teller of a tale in "The Second Hour"; but "Herbert White" had been a teller of a tale, and Bidart's work generally is filled with acts of complex narration. Bidart's presence in the poem does not here depend, as it did in other poems, perhaps especially in "The First Hour of the Night," on the use of extravagant notation; the voice we name "Bidart's voice" exists more quietly within the other voices—Berlioz's, Ovid's—and within "voices" (dream, prayer) that seem profoundly unsocial, unspoken.

When, in the last parts of "The Second Hour of the Night" the "I" reemerges, it does so with many of the ambitions and strategies lamented by Charles Altieri and described above. The passage is "direct" and "immediate"; it is as "sincere" as possible, and it seems to be "describing an event as though it is actually taking place" (Altieri 10). In it, Bidart addresses a dead lover (presumably Brainard, though in the harrowing scene that precedes he, Bidart, sees all of his lovers form a portrait and, in doing so, reveal themselves to be "the same," each one identical to the others) and invites him to "borrow, inhabit my body":

When I look I can see my body
away from me, sleeping.

I say *Yes.* Then you enter it

like a shudder as if eager again to know
what it is to move within arms and legs.

I thought, *I know that he will return it.*

trusted in that none
earlier, none other.

(*Desire* 58)

The strange beauty of this scene arises partly from the wish, a
new one in Bidart, to see someone else—an other—play him; a
fascinating way, in a career of playing others, for Frank Bidart to
end a poem about the difficult necessity of playing himself.

In Bidart we find "confessions" of taboo behaviors, transgressive emotions, wishes for ill fates to fall on the innocent, nar-
cissisms so extreme they replace the world; these confessions are
urgent, even histrionic, "spoken" rather than written, "sincere."
But by and large they are put in the mouths of others, embedded
in texts by others. This desire to retrieve voice from text is not
itself new, having been learned from Frost and Brower, but its
application in Bidart could not have been foreseen. His poems
make us aware of the mingled energies of voice and printed word
and, in doing so, renew some of the richest problems that lyric
poetry puts to itself.

The Tenses of Frank O'Hara

The Present Tense

The poems of Frank O'Hara are distinguished by their exuberance, their conversational rapidity, and their humor. Set beside the poems of his contemporaries these qualities seem especially striking. The dominant poetic modes of the 1950s were, as almost everyone would agree, the opposed poles of Robert Lowell and Allen Ginsberg—"paleface" and "redskin" to employ Phillip Rahv's embarrassing categories, or (in Lévi-Strauss's terms) "the cooked" and "the raw." You were either uptown like Lowell or downtown like Ginsberg; confessional or vatic; WASP or Jew. O'Hara was off the grid—a Greenwich Village jester who nevertheless became a curator at the Museum of Modern Art (MoMA), a Harvard graduate from the farm town of Grafton, Massachusetts, an ex-Catholic, a spirit seemingly free of Lowell's personal and Ginsberg's political gravitas. His poems ("I-do-this-I-do-that" poems, as he called them) recorded his career through the quotidian, free of the distortions of "art" or any other form of self-seriousness. They were "abstract" in that they embodied action, accident, bustle, like the paintings of his friends Jackson Pollock and Willem de Kooning. You could read O'Hara and hardly know Freud or the Cold War existed.

O'Hara's own personality seems to invite celebration. He was, by all accounts, quick-witted, playful (sometimes, when drunk, wickedly so), loyal, generous; he had a "gift for friendship" as his friend Kenneth Koch has said. Stories about O'Hara tend to have him impudently scoring points off the pretensions of others, "paleface" and "redskin" alike. When Jack Kerouac heckled O'Hara at a reading, shouting "O'Hara, you're ruining American poetry," O'Hara, returning serve, answered, "That's more than you ever did for it!" He was equally unsparing of poetry's "right wing,": O'Hara hated Lowell's "Skunk Hour," that epochal "confessional" poem, which he derided (and in doing so revealed his surprising, but persistent, strain of Puritanism) as voyeuristic and "revolting." At one occasion where he shared the stage with Lowell, O'Hara made a mockery of Lowell's ingrown, Aeschylean intensity by reading a poem ("Lana Turner Has Collapsed!") that he, O'Hara, had written during the ferry ride there.

Cab rides, telephone conversations, brisk walks, and background music play important roles in the usual story of O'Hara's poetics. He not only wrote about such things but often allowed them to determine the span and tone of his poems—giving himself, for example, only the duration of one side of a 33 rpm record, or the downtime before a party started, to write. He is said to have written his mock manifesto "Personism" in an hour, to the playing of a Rachmaninoff concerto. His critics are by and large indulgent of O'Hara's reliance on such arbitrary deadlines for composition, delighting in the glamour of insouciance and arbitrariness as a source of art. Insouciance and arbitrariness seem to some more congenial than "inspiration" or "hard work" or "suffering," those other names people have given to the source of poems. O'Hara seems to such critics to be free of the myths of selfhood that, among other things, require that art begin in a private and (therefore) privileged place. He seems to have found his poems in some common, some democratic area into which anybody could stumble.

These last qualities—the "foundness" of O'Hara's poems, the trace they seem to leave of their own making, their grace under self-generated pressure—have been used to tie him to some of the techniques of contemporary painting, and especially to abstract expressionism. The most thorough account of O'Hara's poetics yet written is Marjorie Perloff's excellent *Frank O'Hara: Poet among Painters*, and David Lehman's group portrait, *The Last Avant-Garde*, argues for the centrality of painting to an understanding of O'Hara's art. O'Hara's own poems frequently refer to painting and painters: the anthology piece "Why I Am Not a Painter" is only the most famous among many such poems. The comparison of O'Hara's poems to the canvases of his painter friends is nearly always made; critics differ only in which painter (de Kooning or Larry Rivers, Jane Freilicher or Fairfield Porter) they choose for the comparison. (Criticism of O'Hara can sometimes resemble the eighteenth- and early nineteenth-century debates over whose poems, Gray's, Collins's, or Goldsmith's, most embodied the "nobility" of a Joshua Reynolds painting.) It is a strange irony that art so theoretically alert, so self-conscious in its aesthetic poise, would provoke a renewal of the quaint critical clichés about the sister arts.

Those comparing O'Hara to the abstract expressionists remark that O'Hara's poems are so laden with data that no one piece of datum attains the condition of meaningfulness. Perloff, citing Viktor Shklovsky, thinks that such excessive facticity leads to a "defamiliarization" of the common world, by which things are stripped to their original condition of perceptual strangeness (Perloff 19). O'Hara's facts become, in this argument, placeholders; just as the brushstrokes in a Franz Kline painting exist in order to demarcate abstract pictorial space, O'Hara's data exist as seismograph readings of sentience. The alternative to seeing O'Hara as an "abstract" poet, free from the bother of denotation, has been to insist that he is a hyperrealist: a chronicler of mid-century New York, a kind of effusive and associative historian. David Lehman supposes that the "solution" to an O'Hara poem lay in hidden correspondences among seemingly random data. Lehman argues that "The Day Lady Died" "includes . . . more of the universe than many more ambitious poems" and that, reading it, "historians a century hence could piece together the New York of [1959], perhaps the way archaeologists use a single fossil to recreate an entire ecosystem" (Lehman 200). Lehman doesn't say what about O'Hara's poem he considers a sign of its lack of ambition, but the implication is that O'Hara's purported nonchalance somehow makes "the universe" reveal itself to him as it doesn't for a poet whose poetics seems more highly wrought. Lehman locates all of the ephemera the poem collects (he finds the "ugly NEW WORLD WRITING" O'Hara buys at the newsstand, June 1959, and discovers that it features Ghanaian writers, just as O'Hara says it does) but he fails to say why the poem would cobble together such materials in the first place.

All of these aspects of O'Hara—his "personality," his impudence, the rapidity of his compositional method, his affinities with the action painters, his love of realia—add up to a style as seemingly aleatory, as open to contingency and swerve, as any in American poetry. It is this quality in O'Hara's work, the aleatory quality, that leads many contemporary poets, many of them still quite young, to name O'Hara as their spiritual predecessor. O'Hara looms perhaps larger over the current scene than any other poet of his generation, larger, certainly, than either Lowell or Ginsberg. Young poets tend to view O'Hara as having uncannily anticipated their own discoveries about language and form, an altogether agreeable way of viewing one's own indebtedness. Of course every innovation of poetic style eventually becomes methodized, but the conversion of O'Hara to method is notable given the seeming freshness and immediacy of his style, its preemptive resistance to systems and methods per se. "O'Hara's poetry has no program and therefore cannot be joined" (Perloff 12), writes John Ashbery; but the very programlessness of O'Hara has been copied by poets wishing to seem, like O'Hara, free of an imaginative (and cognitive and historical and political) a priori.

In emphasizing the aleatory and abstract qualities of O'Hara's poetics, critics have noted his "openness" and "immediacy," thinking, as Perloff does, that "photographs, monuments [and] static memories . . . have no place in [O'Hara's] world." "We can now understand why O'Hara loves the *motion* picture, the *action* painting and all forms of dance," writes Perloff, "since they capture the present rather than the past, the present in all its chaotic splendor" (Perloff 40). In such descriptions of O'Hara's style "the present" is taken to be analogous with "the surface" of an abstract expressionist canvas, where the mingled "push" and "pull" of painterly activity replaces (in Hans Hoffman's words) the "arrangement of objects, one after another, toward a vanishing point" (11); O'Hara's linguistic equivalent of push and pull, again according to Perloff and others, is a poetics where forms of conventional poetic depth—metaphor, symbol, whatever lay behind the signifier—is replaced by rapid motion, from item to item to item, through time. This rapidity of movement in the writer produces a synonymous rapidity in the reader's own movement through the poem and, therefore, in the kinds of reading O'Hara will bear—since, that is, O'Hara's poems present the reader with no significant errands of attention, nothing to parse out or mull over in some antechamber of his mind. O'Hara's work would seem therefore ill-suited for acts of critical interpretation, since it finds its own objects utterly already legible. The only thing to do when faced with a poem by Frank O'Hara, it would seem, is to become O'Hara-like in our reading habits, always breezily moving through one poem and on to another, always in motion.

But in emphasizing these qualities (the rapid, the abstract, the aleatory), critics have had to overlook O'Hara's vexed attraction to acts of sustained attention, quiet acts such as reading or listening to music that depend on longer spans of time for their fulfillment. These meditative events occur surprisingly often in his work and are connected, in his mind, with the past. Writing itself, as I will argue, is such an event, and O'Hara's desire to cast writing as something unlike itself (to make it more like painting than music, more involved with the present than the past, more a scattering than a gathering-up) is a deeply American, indeed an Emersonian, desire. The interest in headlong activity, whether constituted by a brush's unbroken movement across a canvas or by a hurried city walk, is a way of discounting, in advance, the power of memory and introspection; but such pre-emptive choices make O'Hara's work exquisitely susceptible to memory and introspection. A style so steadfastly antilyrical as O'Hara's, likewise, is precisely the one that will reestablish lyricality as an authentic undertaking. O'Hara's I-do-this, I-do-that poems, with their darting movement from this to that, attempt to disperse the weight of his attention over as much of the surface of experience as possible in order to keep that surface from rupturing. He possesses an ice-skater's necessary grace, a way of making movement itself beautiful in relation to its impediments. O'Hara's rapidity of movement should be understood as a strategy of self-protection, a way of staying new, tender, and quick vis-à-vis the present moment, since that present moment constitutes the outermost surface, the surface nearest at hand, of the terrifying or stultifying past. Indeed O'Hara, like the painters he admires, possesses extraordinary resources for making the present moment (and its material analogue, the representational surface of a painting or a poem) a viable element for imaginative commerce; but this desire to "speak only of the present" (as he puts it) betrays a profound emotional connection to, not to say fear of, the past. This is precisely why (as I argue) O'Hara's interest in painting is set explicitly at odds with music, where music, since it unfolds in time, scores the moods, and invokes threatening states of feeling like remorse and longing. The problem posed by the past is solved, we might say, by painting, which obscures every layer of activity from its representational surface but the last and outermost. (This quality of painting is especially apparent in modes of painting, like abstract expressionism, which explicitly allegorize the compositional process.) O'Hara's interest in painting, as I argue here, should be viewed not as a source of aesthetic analogues for poetry, models for its behavior, but rather as a source of thwarted but aesthetically consequential aspirations.

The available accounts of O'Hara's poetics, by denying his poems the range and variety of moods and voices they in fact encompass, deprive him of a believably complex interiority; in doing so they also open the door for an "experimental" poetry too glibly disdainful of the interior life to be purposeful—indeed, to be authentically experimental. The O'Hara who was "depressed anxious sullen" (as he describes himself in one of his many poems called "Poem") has tended to disappear behind the effervescent avant-gardist, the kindly wreck; and the avant-garde poetic made in that image is likewise benign, effusive, and anti-intellectual. "If I stay right here I will eventually get into the newspapers / like Robert Frost" O'Hara writes in "Poeme en Forme du Saw" (428). The prediction proved true, perhaps too true, for O'Hara's reputation is now at roughly the point Frost's was before Randall Jarrell, Lionel Trilling, and others took Frost seriously: though our definition of what constitutes kindliness has shifted (from, in Frost's case, a benignly avuncular folksiness to, in O'Hara's, a gleeful—and proudly gay—optimism), our desire for there to be kindly artists, artists who first of all do no harm, has remained intact.

The Now of Painting and the Then of Music

To understand the status of painting in O'Hara's poetics it is crucial first to see O'Hara's love for painting as the enactment of a preference for one thing, painting, over another, music. It is odd to ask a poet to choose between music and painting, of course; poets, depending both on visual imagery and on the more-or-less musical arrangement of words and sounds, need both. If Stevens could love Cezanne and Bach equally, why should O'Hara have to decide between Larry Rivers and Charlie Parker? In large part it is the logic of self-conscious avant-gardism that determines such polemical choosiness—as Lehman and others have shown, the ethos of collaboration (a defining condition of all avant-gardes) determined that O'Hara would inevitably do the same kind of thing as his friends, and his friends were painters, not musicians. Furthermore, jazz—even the ecstatically modernist bebop of Parker—is an essentially vernacular form, a development out of the vernacular, where midcentury American painting (despite its interest in the Jungian "primitive") seems to have been conceived entirely within the culture of high art. The culture of midcentury painting, then, provided O'Hara both with a model for his poetics and a model for his persona, his way of being as an artist. (His enthusiasm for painting functioned additionally, of course, as a way of unifying his pursuits, with days spent as a curator at MoMA and nights—and lunch hours—writing poems.)

O'Hara's choice of painting as a model for his poetry has about it the deliberateness, as well as the pathos, of a vow. Vows differ from ordinary choices in that they can only be ratified by deliberate and continuous action in the future; vows need the whole of the future in order not to be proven false. Vows require a continuous exertion of will precisely because it is in their nature to fail; a vow of chastity, for example, makes sexual behavior radically purposeful, exchanging an ordinary behavior for a purposefully extraordinary one: the very premise of the vow is that but for the vow, sexual life would lumber sloppily along. The narrative of O'Hara's life involves (as it would have to a degree, perhaps, for any gay man in the nineteen-fifties) sudden birth into, rather than consecutive and steady progression toward, approximate personal freedom; the young O'Hara who played the piano for his aunts in Grafton, Massachusetts, could only suddenly, after the release of long-muffled sexual and creative aspirations, become a mature person and a mature artist. O'Hara's noted aversion to New England ("where I grew / and tried both to fight and to escape" [132]) can be explained in these terms. In such a narrative, recorded music, both for its associations with his early life and for its essential nostalgia, takes on the coloration and pitch of the past, while contemporary painting assumes the energy and full presence of the present. O'Hara's own aesthetics of immediacy finds its visual analogue in the paintings of the New York School, but both kinds of immediacy must be understood as a flight from nostalgia, a flight that can only endure by being constantly reaffirmed. In a late, melancholy poem, O'Hara defines old age as "all day long [sitting] in a window / and [seeing] nothing but the past." Painting in O'Hara is always (to put it another way) painting-instead-of-music, the buzzing emergency of the present over the static, monumental past.

In a 1958 letter to Gregory Corso, O'Hara claims to prefer the "stimulus" of painting to the more fashionable stimulus (for Corso's Beats especially) of jazz. Perloff quotes the letter as proof that "painting . . . had a special place in O'Hara's universe." O'Hara writes:

> I've noticed that what Kerouac and "they" feel as the content of Jazz in relation to their own work (aspirations) I feel about painting. . . . That is where one takes Bird for inspiration I take Bill de Kooning: partly because I think jazz is beautiful enough or too, but not fierce enough, and where jazz is fleeting (in time) and therefore poignant, de K is final and therefore tragic. . . . Then also, I don't have to see what I admire while I'm writing and would rather not hear it. . . . Maybe I should try to give a reading somewhere in front of a Pollock or a de K. . . . I guess my point is that painting doesn't intrude on poetry. (Perloff 110)

"To give a poetry reading in front of a de Kooning," Perloff delightedly comments, "this is the kind of aspiration we expect from O'Hara" (Perloff 110). But in "To Larry Rivers" O'Hara dismisses a similar idea on the grounds that the "drone" of poetry couldn't compete against such a backdrop. Here is the poem in its entirety:

> You are worried that you don't write?
> Don't be. It's the tribute of the air that
> your paintings don't just let go
> of you. And what poet ever sat down
> in front of a Titian, pulled out
> his versifying tablet and began
> to drone? Don't complain, my dear.
> You do what I can only name.
>
> (128)

This envy of painterly "doing"—action rather than mere description—is at the heart of O'Hara's desire to find for painting a verbal analogue in poems. While descriptive language, even of the impressionistic variety practiced by O'Hara in his art criticism, can never bridge the gap between signifier and signified, "poetic" language purportedly can. The notion that a lyric poem, if organized properly, might convey the experience of seeing a Larry Rivers painting better than descriptive prose is not, in itself, surprising; what is surprising is the insistence on some critics' part that the new means of painting explored by the New York School might necessitate not just an analogous but also a synonymous newness in O'Hara's poems. O'Hara's poems, by this argument, can be made not merely to "look" (that is, rather than "sound") but furthermore to "look like a Rivers" (or a de Kooning or a Titian).

Perloff treats O'Hara's poem "Joseph Cornell" as an example of this verbal "approximation" of visual forms. Cornell's surrealist "boxes"—three-dimensional, glass-encased rectangles that suggest both paintings and windows—inspire the poem's own rigid rectangularity:

> Into a sweeping meticulously-
> detailed disaster the violet
> light pours. It's not a sky,
> it's a room. And in the open
> field a glass of absinthe is
> fluttering its song of India.
> Prairie winds circle mosques.
> You are always a little too
> young to understand. He is
> bored with his sense of the
> past the artist. Out of the
> prescient rock in his heart
> he has spread a land without
> flowers of near distances.
>
> (237)

"Joseph Cornell" surrenders the expressive possibilities of more conventional lineation—lineation according, say, to metrical or phrasal necessity—in order to look as much as possible like a

Cornell box. But it must be noted that the poem is also, self-consciously, a kind of sonnet. It is fourteen lines long (though narrower across the line than a traditional sonnet) and breaks rhetorically, if not numerically, into "octave" and "sestet." The wit of the poem depends precisely on such literary family resemblance, which comes to seem inevitable despite the poem's own attempts to escape the closed circuit of linguistic interpenetration. Cornell's boxes were the shape of paintings because, it might be said, paintings are the shape of windows, and so on and so on: ultimately the rectangular dimensions of the human body are probably accountable for a painting's normative rectangularity. But why should a Cornell box be three dimensional, precisely unlike paintings? The expansion of painting's dimensions leads, in Cornell, to a deep and previously inaccessible insight about the conventional dimensions of painting. We are never more conscious of the strange illusionistic power of conventional two-dimensional painting than when looking into the actual depths of a Cornell box. Likewise, O'Hara's right margin, though Procrustean (two lines in a row, for example, are broken after the definite article) bring him full-circle to the precise shape of the oldest and most canonical English form. Cornell's boxes (especially when considered beside the art of his contemporaries) seem, finally, to be engaged with very old-fashioned forms of beauty: the night sky or a fragmented landscape, scenes often seen through little windows cut into the pictorial space. His work, unlike that of, say Kline, has been called "intimate" and "nostalgic" (Solomon 5). The beauty of O'Hara's poem, likewise, lay in the, for him, uncharacteristic lushness of scenic phrases like "flowers of near distances" or "Prairie winds circle mosques." Something about the severity of the box, its nonnegotiable rectangularity, inspires Cornell to seek out a literal (not illusionistic or conventional) depth of field; the same impulse leads O'Hara to a descriptive elegance and a slowness of phrasing that is otherwise rare in his work. Such linguistic techniques suggest a range of "literary," even Shakespearean, expressive strategies, where O'Hara's usual language suggests naïveté and two-dimensional immediacy.

While the visual analogue of Cornell's boxes adds, to "Joseph Cornell," another dimension of *ekphrasis*, it seems strange to call the poem a "translation" of Cornell, as Perloff does. The salient feature of Cornell's work cannot be its rectangularity, when rectangularity is the very feature his boxes share with ordinary two-dimensional paintings; and the rectangularity of the boxes is their only spatial quality that O'Hara's poem is capable of reproducing. "Joseph Cornell" is therefore no more a "translation" of Cornell than the pictograms of the Metaphysicals are translations of swans and altarpieces. Much of the interpretation of O'Hara's visual "approximations" is crippled by overstatement, and the overstatement can usually be attributed to an evangelical wish on the critic's part to take the rhetoric of the avant-garde as scriptural fact. O'Hara was himself cautious around such rhetoric. For him the dejection at the end of "To Larry Rivers" makes up the ground note of all explorations of the verbal approximation of visual effects. The failure of such experiments is their very premise; for O'Hara, when language tries to loosen the yoke of referentiality, it takes on a tragic dimension. O'Hara knows that spatial effects, in Rivers's or Cornell's media, are after all literally possible—while in language they can only be approximated. "To give a poetry reading in front of a de Kooning," then, would only underscore the salient differences between poetry and painting—differences that O'Hara suggests, in a self-effacing mood, function to the detriment of his own medium. O'Hara's word "versifying" implies a mechanical and dilettantish kind of art, against the almost tidal power of the Titian; "drone" is a word that characterizes, for O'Hara, the default tone of poetry at its worst—colorlessly bleak, monotonous. These same qualities are attributed, in another poem, to some background music playing in O'Hara's apartment:

Why do you play such dreary music
on Saturday afternoon, when tired
mortally tired I long for a little
reminder of immortal energy?
          All

week long while I trudge fatiguingly
from desk to desk in the museum
you spill your miracles of Grieg
and Honegger on shut-ins.
                              Am I not
shut in too, and after a week
of work don't I deserve Prokofieff?

Well, I have my beautiful de Kooning
to aspire to. I think it has an orange
bed in it, more than the ear can hold.
                              (210)

The imagination, O'Hara thinks, can explore its own changes
and variations over the image of a "beautiful de Kooning"; music,
especially the dirgelike "dreary" music on the radio, by comparison scores the imagination according to its own prerogatives. It
is in the nature of music to "spill" into consciousness, entering
involuntarily, and remaining there throughout a span of its own,
and no one else's, determination. The "Radio" of this poem is
played by someone else; the music will stop only when O'Hara
("mortally tired") musters the persuasive energy to convince his
friend to stop it. In the meantime, an abstract visual image, de
Kooning's near-bed, provides the only means of transport. That
it should be almost a bed, of course, implies that there is something in its way of being visual, as well as its way of being abstract,
just out of focus (and, unlike the music of Grieg, neutral in terms
of mood), that acts as a consolation and a haven.

   "Radio" is of course first and foremost a poem about the excru-
ciations of a hangover, but it suggests, lightly, that consciousness
itself "hurts" the way a hangover does. Meditation on the "beautiful de Kooning," then, negates the "dreary" and lugubrious music
spilling into the immediate sensible world. The word "aspiration"
implies a serial act, one that intensifies through time but that,
since it is absorptive rather than expansive, suspends time. It is
the very fixity of the de Kooning, its permanence in time, that
allows the person viewing or imagining it to "aspire," to undertake an imaginative act that depends on time to be completed.

Poems that aspire to be like painting, likewise, acknowledge in a deep way the futility of such aspirations, doing so in the very dimension, time, that is inaccessible to the visual arts. "Why I Am Not a Painter" is O'Hara's most famous statement on this topic, but one that (as Perloff and others have shown) as a statement ends up being maddeningly evasive. The poem, Perloff thinks, is a "profound jest": "If someone asks a stupid question, O'Hara implies, he deserves a stupid answer" (Perloff 98). Indeed "Why I Am Not a Painter" does seem, from its title forward, to strike an intentionally naive tone, as though stooping to someone's level. As a structure, though, the poem is a virtual dictionary of explicatory gestures—seeming to take its nagging question utterly literally and seriously and offering a parable that, while by no means clear or simple, is nevertheless thought-provoking. If it is a "stupid answer," it is a brilliantly stupid one, one that manages, under the cloak of irony, to say something in response to a question that probably ought to engender only a blank stare.

"Why I Am Not a Painter" opens with a seemingly bland announcement of the obvious:

> I am not a painter, I am a poet.
> Why? I think I would rather be
> a painter, but I am not.
>
> (262)

The most viable "answer" to the question is perhaps given in the poem's first line; the remainder of the poem borrows that line's matter-of-fact authority to consolidate its considerable imaginative and expressive freedom. Questions with no correct answers are just the ones that interest poets, especially poets like O'Hara with a taste for indeterminacy. But these opening lines also convey the sense of a mental stammer—as though all that could be "done" with the question at the outset is to restate its premise. The parable that serves to answer the question does so as a substitute for the straight answer and is launched with the defeated interjection, "Well, for instance." The first half of the parable concerns the "painter," where the second will turn to the poet. Here is the first:

> Well,
>
> for instance, Mike Goldberg
> is starting a painting. I drop in.
> "Sit down and have a drink" he
> says. I drink; we drink. I look
> up. "You have SARDINES. in it."
> "Yes, it needed something there."
> "Oh." I go and the days go by
> and I drop in again. The painting
> is going on, and I go, and the days
> go by. I drop in. The painting is
> finished. "Where's SARDINES?"
> All that's left is just
> letters, "It was too much," Mike says.
>
> (262)

The artistic process, no matter what the medium, is likely to look irrational and insouciant when watched from the outside; but the enjambment of "The painting is / finished" underscores O'Hara's shock that, while he was dumbly going from place to place, dropping in and out of Goldberg's studio, a painting was taking shape. The painting happens, as Hemingway said of bankruptcy, "gradually then all at once"; it is completed as much, in the end, by subtraction as by accretion; and whatever its aesthetic affiliations may be, it will not hold itself to a standard of representational meaning. "SARDINES" embodies, perhaps, the very essence of referentiality, a word with no abstract or metaphorical content whatsoever, a word whose "meaning" cannot but come vividly to life: one's fingers and lips get oily at the very mention of "sardines." Of course the presence of "SARDINES"—all capitals— on the surface of a painting changes the word's representational status; in such a highly self-conscious visual context any word, no matter how swiftly denotative, will probably dissolve into its

constituent lines and angles, and the more concrete in signifi-
cation, the more likely that, in so dissolving, it might point out
some important differences between linguistic and visual "meaning." When we find out later that the finished painting, though
it contains no sardines, is titled "Sardines," we conclude that
"completion" confers on the artwork the status of objective, noncontingent materiality, making it as hard and real as a can of
sardines, and perhaps just as prone, as a commodity in the art
market, to the sort of indignities real sardines suffer.

The problem of interpreting this parable of the sardines as I
have above, however, is that in doing so the critic must ignore the
tonal qualities—the nonchalance, the wit, the self-mockery—of
O'Hara's delivery. The parable is offered, to begin with, tenta-
tively, in place of a "straight answer" or failed axiomatic proof.
O'Hara's comic comings and goings, the capacity of his voice
to modulate into mock horror or disbelief, his impression of a
deadpan Goldberg ("It needed something there") are all at least
as important as the data—canvas and painter, studio, "subject
matter"—that the parable employs. The same could be said of
the counterparable of poetic composition that follows:

> But me? One day I am thinking of
> a color: orange. I write a line
> about orange. Pretty soon it is a
> whole page of words, not lines.
> Then another page. There should be
> so much more, not of orange, of
> words, of how terrible orange is
> and life. Days go by. It is even in
> prose, I am a real poet. My poem
> is finished and I haven't mentioned
> orange yet.
>
> (262)

O'Hara suggests several distinctions between poetry and painting: the poet, according to this account, has recourse to metaphor,
and his movement into and through metaphor must always chart
itself against human coordinates (not just "how terrible orange

is" but also the terribleness of "life") where the painter can act in the interest of "pure" compositional necessity ("It needed something there"). The sense that referentiality itself is to blame for the tragic element in poetry—that linguistic naming is built on exile and desire—is suggested by the movement from "orange" to "words" to "how terrible orange is, and life," as though linguistic practice were itself bound up with sorrow. O'Hara's painter, by comparison, stands back from his canvas, crosses his arms, and says "Voila!" O'Hara's poem, we learn, is called "Oranges," though it contains no reference to them; likewise, Goldberg's abstract painting is called "Sardines."

To read the poem as statement as I have done above, though, ignores the gestural excess beyond statement that so characterizes the poem. "Why I Am Not a Painter" is a map not merely of the successful and resolved thought but also the aborted or partial thought: O'Hara's erasures, unlike those of Goldberg, leave a trace. The best answer to the poem's title question, then, is not any one position taken or refuted by the poem but the poem itself, its own unfolding performance. Where a canvas can only record the path taken by gesture—the path the body makes over the surface of the canvas—a poem can record the affective content of a span of time, what it felt like to make the work of art. Painters can suggest states of feeling, of course (Pollock seems exuberant, de Kooning seems angry, and so on and so on) but only writers can say precisely how it is with them. The poem, then, though it won't name the difference between the visual and the verbal arts, enacts that difference with its complex affective surface. Statements that might otherwise seem banal ("life is terrible") come here to seem inevitable. Possibly the statement "life is terrible" is only viable within a lyric poem, at this moment in history, if it is subordinated to the statement "orange is terrible."

When O'Hara speaks of the "poignancy" of music, then, we might assume that it is music's proximity to poetry, its proximity to his poetry, that keeps O'Hara from embracing its influence or aspiring to its condition. We might say even that O'Hara's poems, where they approach painterly effects or treat paintings or painters as their subjects, do so as a kind of devotional act—an act founded on the impossibility of its own consummation. The emotional consequences of the differing categories between the arts of time and the arts of space might once have been figured as those of the distance between man and God. There is no way for de Kooning's bed to answer back to O'Hara's poem; O'Hara's name is not in its language. The various solutions suggested for this problem—poetry readings in front of paintings or paintings that include the words of poets as a part of their compositional surface—tend only to make the postures of the sister arts, vis-à-vis one another, look more rigid and tend to expose the banalities of each. Where painting is concerned, poetry can only stand by and watch; but the desire to "be like a Cornell box" or to "concentrate on a de Kooning painting"—or to answer an unanswerable question—creates a task for poetic language, forcing it into deliberate action.

Prospective-Retrospective Elegy

The function of memory in O'Hara is best explored in relation to his poems of pure incident, what he called I-do-this, I-do-that poems. All of the poems I discuss above are at least nominally organized around a problem (How does painterly composition differ from poetic composition? What sort of music soothes a hangover?) that, though it cannot entirely rein in O'Hara's performance, nevertheless provides for it a plausible arena. His real innovation, though (as Helen Vendler has suggested) is the poem whose own course is entirely coincident with the course of its protagonist (*Part* 179). "A poem is a walk," says A. R. Ammons (Burr 12); if so, O'Hara's I-do-this, I-do-that poems are a brisk, distracted walk through New York, spiky with perceptual events. This sort of walk is distinguished by sudden changes of perceptual, and sometimes emotional, course; the Wordsworthian walk, with its long expanses, its huge sight lines, suggests a poetry of contemplation, all the more so for the rare, unexpected vistas that suddenly disable contemplation. Ammons himself prefers walks in which sights wash into consciousness and then, like surf, slowly recede back into the mass of unintelligibility. Ammons is the poet of porous consciousness, of the mind that detects new flora and fauna in its own backyard or along familiar pathways. Ammons, like Jorie Graham, is always "finding himself" in the Emersonian sense, as though waking into the phenomenal world. In each of these poets, the walk, besides being "a poem," is also a model for epistemology, for the way the mind plots its errands into and back from its own wilderness. But O'Hara has no interest in epistemology; his walk poems are the least cerebral such poems since Whitman's. O'Hara like Whitman seeks "the actual," which precisely means that which is too noisy and near to be contemplated, that which makes itself immediately known. His attention span is scant; he is the American poet whom it is hardest to picture reading a book.

"The Day Lady Died," an elegy for Billie Holiday, is one of O'Hara's most widely anthologized poems, in part because it provides such a memorable example of the I-do-this, I-do-that method. In summarizing the poem, in fact, one finds oneself inadvertently parsing O'Hara's normative structures. The poem records a walk through the streets of New York, preserving the minute coordinates of that walk: it is not only "1959" but also "12:20" and a "Friday," "three days after Bastille day." This kind of detail creates a strange sense of diminishing returns—the day is filled with ordinary temporal dramas, small daily bits of significance, and is therefore more or less interchangeable with any other day. The poem occurs in the present tense, in what might be called the blank present tense, the tense of doing errands or getting lunch. The only futurity such a state knows is the immediate deadline, the lunch hour or the train schedule; the only past available to it is the past of the calendar—insignificant holidays, the meaningless events of the work week:

> It is 12:20 in New York a Friday
> three days after Bastille day, yes
> it is 1959 and I go get a shoeshine
> because I will get off the 4:19 in Easthampton

at 7:15 and then go straight to dinner
and I don't know the people who will feed me.

(325)

What is true of time is equally true of place. The New York of
this poem is set exactly at body temperature, so to speak; it is an
element seemingly incapable of providing cognitive or emotional
surprise. It has cognitive and emotional content, of course; it is
not mere data. But that content never strays very far above or
below the horizon line of ordinary thought. The poem is a map
of local, utterly manageable disturbances of equilibrium of the
kind that average out to "normal."

But this day is not a "normal" day, as O'Hara's title warns us;
the day participates both in the horizontal progress of days, where
July 17 follows July 16 and precedes July 18, where Friday follows
Thursday, where a fixed number of tasks must be finished before
the lunch hour ends, while at the same time participating in a
kind of vertical order of days inaugurated by the death of Billie
Holiday. The poem records not just the event of Billie Holliday's
death but everything adjacent to that event, as though through
a wide-angle lens. Ordinary life, the quotidian lunch-hour walk,
is revealed as a minor theater of affect, as O'Hara weighs in
about the cover of the latest *New World Writing* ("ugly") and the
haughtiness of the bank teller ("Miss Stillwagon . . . doesn't even
look up my balance for once in her life").

O'Hara's own word for his errand, buying magazines and
lunch and liquor and cigarettes, is "casual," meaning "rote" and
"uneventful." The poem continues:

then I go back where I came from to 6th Avenue
and the tobacconist in the Ziegfeld Theatre and
casually ask for a carton of Gauloises and a carton
of Picayunes.

(325)

"Casual" is a Yeatsian word, and since it is so importantly placed
in O'Hara it is worthwhile pausing to consider its Yeatsian

echoes. One of the great poetic meditations on time is Yeats's poem "Easter 1916," which commemorates the Irish Nationalist uprising on Easter Sunday, 1916. The poem, in insistent trimeter, is punctuated by the arresting refrain "A terrible beauty is born." This formal dynamic is the correlative of the poem's deepest topic, namely, the question of how meaning becomes suddenly affixed to "meaningless" ordinary lives as the private life is transformed by political commitment, by what Yeats calls "sacrifice." The poem sees the courtesies and traumas of everyday life under the sign of history, as though "Easter 1916" had been, for all of its participants, a kind of unheard music playing all this time underneath the quotidian:

> I have met them at close of day
> Coming with vivid faces
> From counter or desk among grey
> Eighteenth-century houses.
> I have passed with a nod of the head
> Or polite meaningless words,
> Or have lingered awhile and said
> Polite meaningless words,
> And thought before I had done
> Of a mocking tale or a gibe
> To please a companion
> Around the fire at the club,
> Being certain that they and I
> But lived where motley is worn:
> All changed, changed utterly:
> A terrible beauty is born.
>   (*Collected Poems* 177)

Yeats, like O'Hara, sees ordinary time as marked by insignificant vacillation, what might commonly be called "comings and goings," where human presence seems quaint, purposeless, "lingering." Like O'Hara, Yeats is interested in the ways within ordinary time that the sharps of affect ("a mocking tale or a gibe") are played against the flats of routine: such fleeting performances of self testify to the temporary imperceptibility of time or, perhaps, to the ways time can be made (fleetingly) imperceptible. Within this temporal element not only tales and gibes but also idle chitchat ("polite meaningless words") and acts of minimal recognition ("a nod of the head") are possible, implying a porous, a merely loosely bound community.

Where "Easter 1916" takes a recollective stance vis-à-vis the quotidian, "The Day Lady Died" tries as much as possible to seem immersed in it; Yeats's poem is formal and severe in its organization, where O'Hara's, true to its own terms, is "casual," small in its body, incapable of axiomatic statement. But just as "Easter 1916" is capable of self-chastisement so too is "The Day Lady Died." Yeats fears that the rigidity of his aesthetic stance may constitute just the sort of "sacrifice" that will "make a stone of the heart": a clenched and obstinate cast of mind, whether manifested in a political slogan or a poetic refrain, he fears, is at odds with an authentic emotional life, a life capable of sympathetic, and imaginative, extension. "Easter 1916" becomes one of Yeats's great statements about the imagination precisely by including itself, its own unfolding performance, under its most searing indictment; O'Hara, likewise, arrives at an imaginative fullness and viability by seeing his own style as, despite itself, culpable. O'Hara's poem can be seen as an attempt to incapacitate the faculty of memory, and all of its attendant threats, by radically shortening one's span of attention: the sense in the poem of being under the pressure of time (it is Friday afternoon, there are trains to catch and shoes to shine) provides the poem's presiding fiction, according to which there is only time to process the outer surface of the world (labels, magazine covers) before having to move on to the next event and then the next. But this outermost surface, O'Hara learns, can also be meaningful, even shockingly so. The poem concludes with the act of reading a headline announcing the death of Billie Holliday:

> and a NEW YORK POST with her face on it
> and I am sweating a lot by now and thinking of
> leaning on the john door in the 5 SPOT

while she whispered a song along the keyboard
to Mal Waldron and everyone and I stopped breathing.

(325)

The poem, which has been explicitly about encountering (from
O'Hara's perspective and from our own) signs whose content is
unsurprising ("PARK LANE," "STREGA," "NEW WORLD WRITING"),
introduces a new sign ("NEW YORK POST") whose content takes
our breath away. All of the perceptual events preceding this last
one are revealed by it to be insufficiently meaningful to constitute
all by themselves a "day" or, for that matter, a "poem." The very
moment the poem finds its subject, furthermore, it finds also its
genre (elegy) its exemplary gestures (leaning against a bathroom
door, whispering, playing the piano), and its notion of beauty
(Billie Holliday singing.) It finds these elements in the past,
that region from which it considered itself to be fully insulated.
Magically, the black and white of a newspaper headline changes
to Mal Waldron's piano keyboard.

Since "The Day Lady Died" ends with a loss of breath, the
poem should be described not only as an elegy but additionally as
a self-elegy; and since, at the very moment it is describing a loss
of breath (both "mine" and "everyone's"), it forces its readers to
"lose" their breath in order to honor the silence indicated by the
white of the page, it becomes our elegy as well. These coin-
ciding deaths, Holliday's, O'Hara's, "everyone's," our own, make
"The Day Lady Died" an example of what I would call O'Hara's
collaborative autobiography, a sense that the self is constituted
not apart from social life but precisely within, and between,
friends.

If we all die simultaneously, as in "The Day Lady Died," then
working backward it is safe to assume that we live that way as well.
The simultaneity of engaged friendship, where (as Robert Lowell
says) everyone seems to live "the same life" is O'Hara's model for
selfhood, a model that prefers accident to essence, composite
to singular. This averaging of selfhood, where poetry is enlisted
to describe only what might plausibly happen between friends,

in the social world of perceptual fact and sociability rather than in the rarefied confines of any one private world, is theorized in O'Hara's often-ironic manifesto "Personism," with its remark "[I realized] I could use the telephone instead of writing the poem." With "Personism," O'Hara states, "The poem is at last between two persons instead of two pages" (499). These statements are often read, rightly, as indicating O'Hara's interest in intimate scale, the scale represented by one-on-one conversation between people close enough to talk at length, freely, on the telephone. But additionally they suggest the status of poetry as an average, a point where two claims or interests meet. Of course O'Hara's poems are emphatically personal, but they are remarkable for their ability to situate themselves, as he says, "between" friends. The notion of poetry as telephone conversation implies, then, not just intimacy of tone but commonality of reference, an art of the near at hand and common.

And yet, as I have been arguing in this chapter, O'Hara's poems often read like failed experiments, staged dramatically. Their desire to live only in the present, or perhaps in the extended present, which includes the imminent future and the immediate past, is bound to fail: in part because of the generic predisposition of lyric poetry for acts of long, transcendent memory and in part because of the tendency of anything so scrupulously repressed to turn from potential to kinetic energy. It is memory, then, that finally haunts O'Hara the most and that becomes his most profound topic. "Ave Maria" is O'Hara's poem about growing old and about the fond dream of dismantling preemptively the chilling tableaux of memory and remorse that seem, to this perpetually youthful poet, to compose old age. It begins with a charming injunction:

> Mothers of America
>   let your kids go to the movies!
> get them out of the house so they won't know what you're up to
> it's true that fresh air is good for the body

but what about the soul
that grows in darkness, embossed by silvery images.

(372)

The note struck by "they won't know what you're up to" is one of
the poem's most important, since it sets up adulthood (or at the
very least straight adulthood) as synonymous with secrecy and
dishonesty. The stifling interiors of the home are contrasted with
the vistas of the movies, their ability to transport us to "glamorous
countries" far from home, and with the apartment of a "pleasant
stranger." Your children, O'Hara continues,

may even be grateful to you
                    for their first sexual experience
which only cost you a quarter
                    and didn't upset the peaceful home
they will know where candybars come from
                    and gratuitous bags of popcorn
as gratuitous as leaving the movie before it's over
with a pleasant stranger whose apartment is in the Heaven on
    Earth Bldg
near the Williamsburg Bridge.

(372)

This is a vision of the movies, familiarly, as a means of escape,
but also as a crucible for the reformulation of identity, as we pass
from "peaceful home" to "stranger's apartment," from the world
of lugubrious, maladroit parental instruction (where babies come
from) to the ebullient world of erotic instruction (where candybars and gratuitous bags of popcorn come from). It is a poem, of
course, about coming out of the closet, about exchanging one's
parents' home for one's lover's and, perhaps, about exchanging
one's parents for the surrogate domesticity, full of delights, that
a stranger offers. But the immense pressure, the urgency of these
injunctions, is being applied not from the point of view of the
present but from that of the future. The poem ends with a harrowing prophecy of what the future holds for those kids whose

parents bullied them into staying home and staying within all of
the constructs of identity that "home" implies:

> so don't blame me if you won't take this advice
> and the family breaks up
> and your children grow old and blind in front of the TV set
> seeing
> movies you wouldn't let them see when they were young.
>
> (372)

The notion here is that movies that one could not see, when
young, end up "seeing" us when we are old, in the grotesquely
miniaturized and domesticated form of the TV. The mortifica-
tion and shame of old age, itself a spectacle, replaces the "glamorous countries" of one's youth. The poem is a kind of warning
against forms of memory that are saturated with remorse and
longing, an ingenious (but of course doomed) stay against such
memory. Far from being immersed in the present, far from being
a parable about the present as a means of escape, "Ave Maria" is
a poem that sees the present from the point of view of the distant future, and it is this future-perfect imaginative act, this looking forward to looking backward, which governs its urgent injunctions.

In poetry, David Bromwich writes, "an intense retrospect is the
result of an earlier unseeing" (Bromwich 20). O'Hara's poems of
the present tense portray the inverse phenomenon: vision so thorough that it comes to seem like archival substantiation, as though
someone in the future was always waiting for us, saying "Prove
that you existed." O'Hara's sense of the present might therefore
be called prospective-retrospective. This immersion in what will
have been, I would argue, is the defining tendency of O'Hara's
work, a tendency that when understood gives a new shape and
purpose even to his most radically present-tense poems. The
obliteration of the immediate and near at hand that memory and
nostalgia represent is, O'Hara knows, inevitable. But in his emphatic record keeping of the immediate and near at hand he can
create, for us, the illusion of nearness and contemporaneity—as

well as its subsequent evaporation, as we move through time farther and farther from where O'Hara stands.

Why call O'Hara an autobiographical poet at all, when his poems have been invoked so often to repudiate the conventions of autobiography? His aesthetic strategies, like Bishop's, are best seen as displacements of the personal onto sturdier, more objective sites—not because one's autobiography is inevitable as a poetic subject, though in a very loose sense, I believe that it is but, rather, because O'Hara's poems reveal, in their intensely personal tones, their intimacy of address, and their vivid "actual" world of reference, a desire to represent "what happened" to one man as his life unfolded. But in this formulation both "what happened" and "one man" must be qualified, for O'Hara's poetry is, I believe, a record of common events in the life of a man whose primary energies were toward friendship, social life, collaboration. O'Hara's autobiography is not, like Ashbery's, anybody's, but nor does it belong (as Lowell's does) to one man and one man alone. This sense of intimate life as bound up with the lives and fates of others and of personality as somehow a collaboration will be developed later, as I will argue, by Louise Glück.

Forms of Narrative in the Poetry of Louise Glück

Louise Glück is the author of ten books of poetry from *Firstborn* (1968) to *Averno* (2006) and a book of essays, *Proofs and Theories* (1995). Glück's poetry has been well known for over thirty-five years, and many adjectives have been used to describe it: "disaffected or angry" (*EB online*) and, more recently, "spare and elegant" (Hass). Her most recent books call for a new set of adjectives: these books (I shall focus on *Meadowlands* and *Averno* here) show Glück as amply social, funny, and tender as often as she is stern, dispassionate, and ironic. This broader affective range is the result, as I will argue here, of her interest in narrative. The opportunities presented by telling stories—and the frustrations with having stories told about her—these have become, I think, central concerns for Glück. No living poet has made lyric poetry answer so fruitfully to the narrative drive.

Glück writes poems of alternating ecstasy and self-repudiation. Her fineness of feeling takes her very far into experience, where often she finds the impetus for sudden, rapid retreat. But her poems (more and more as she has developed) also anticipate their own perceptual, emotional, and spiritual peril and are built ingeniously to stave off that peril. The resulting poetry has been a deliberate, meticulous taking in of more and more world, through a lens that once seemed too narrow for panorama, governed by a sensibility that seemed too rarefied for what Whitman calls "the pulling and hauling" of ordinary life.

Her various aesthetic strategies are all designed for one purpose, to protect her fineness of perception and exactness of speech from what it cannot but see and cannot but say. She is aware of the limits of this sensibility (which would seem to prize expertise over imagination, the domestic over the prophetic, the aesthetic over the "real") and has endeavored to expand those limits while keeping the center intact. Her poems are as "personal" as anyone's, indeed fiercely so, but their medium is strangely impersonal, even generic: written, often, from a slightly distanced point of view or written from a point of view that craves such distance. She likes coolness not for its own sake but for the sake of intellect, which cannot thrive nearer its objects. The simplest description of her would be "ironic," which is just how she has her dissatisfied husband describe her in her book-length sequence *Meadowlands*:

> Mommy's too ironic. She wouldn't
> do a rhumba in the driveway.
>
> (40)

But "irony" here is a failed, because self-ennobling, description. It is what the husband might say to permit his own ongoing coarseness of perception. Glück's poems are filled with these moments where the vanity or fear in others distorts their perception of her. In "Prism," she presents self-description not as her inalienable right but as an irritating necessity given others' misperceptions. The base of her voice is this sometimes stern, often amused, always meticulous correction.

For a writer so suspicious of the capacity of language to insulate people from perception and its consequences, lyric poetry is an odd choice of genre. For a writer who prizes directness of speech and affect, too, it seems unpromising. Anyone who begins with these biases will err, when she sometimes errs, on the side of asceticism. This quality of withholding, of refusing to indulge, conventional forms of lyric satisfaction is Glück's most remarked aspect.

For Nick Halpern (writing in *Domestic and Prophetic*), the essential note in Glück is "disgust" or "revulsion," a note first struck in her early poem "The Chicago Train." In that poem, staged in a stalled subway, we see a repulsive family at close range, the mother's crotch "pulsing," her sleeping baby's hair filled with lice. "Her disgust is not preliminary," writes Halpern, "not staged so as to be corrected. Nor can it be disowned: it is not deflected onto a speaker in a dramatic monologue. The speaker is confident that we will feel, that we already feel, even though her disgust is directed towards subjects (a family on a train, in some sense 'the family of man') towards whom most readers do not like to feel they could experience revulsion" (232). Glück's asceticism amounts (in this account) to a desire, quite simply, not to have lice. We all want not to have lice, but few of us would choose to write a poem that demonstrates this wish so forcefully. Her later tones of intellectual and philosophical abstraction, her "mature" style, would seem to be one in which she has stopped taking train rides altogether.

Halpern rightly points out that the usual lyric poem about such an experience would find some means (affectual, linguistic, imagistic) to atone for its own revulsion; we would not be left alone (as in this poem we are) to ponder the revulsion we were instructed to feel. And yet for me, and I suspect for Glück, this poem offers too much artificial consolation for the disgust it occasions. Indeed this poem is rife with gestures Glück later abandons: in it we find street slang à la Lowell, phonetic and sonic play à la Plath, an abruptly "shocking" conclusion à la James Wright. Here, with the borrowed gestures italicized, is "The Chicago Train":

> Across from me the whole ride
> Hardly stirred: just *Mister* with his *barren*
> *Skull* across the arm-rest while *the kid*
> Got his head between his *mama's* legs and slept. *The poison*

That replaces air took over.
And they sat—as though paralysis preceding death
Had nailed them there. The track bent south.
I saw her pulsing crotch . . . the lice rooted in that baby's hair.
                                                        (*First Four* 5)

"Mister," "mamma," "the kid" all attempt sly idiomatic parody, something Glück will later never do. The abrupt line breaks ("barren / Skull") and epigrammatic descriptions ("The poison / That replaces air took over") are tried-and-true methods for making the demotic voice strain against the necessities of form and genre. The last line, with its hideous observation, seems more hysterical than actual, proportionally wrong coming from a voice that has spent long enough on subways to know the "street" slang of "mister," "mamma," and "the kid." "The Chicago Train" is a poem written by someone who thinks of seeing X and putting X into language as two distinct stages of composing a poem—so much so that she can render what she sees in borrowed language. Glück will later find ways of making seeing and writing seem simultaneous and of eliminating from her poems any linguistic excess that blurs her sight.

The language of "The Chicago Train," for all its vividness and specificity and immediacy, seeks to give objective shape to what is a radically, and therefore dismissibly, subjective experience. The poem does not, as Halpern claims, leave us bracingly alone with our disgust; rather it seeks to transform that disgust into a "Poem" with a capital *P*. The "poem with a capital *P*" at large in the world, circa 1968, was of course the mannered late-confessional poem. Glück knows better than to add undue allegorical or mythic weight to that lousy baby, but she doesn't yet know quite how to avoid adding linguistic and affectual weight. When (in her second book) she discovers a new, simple, almost molecular style, she jettisons the kinds of words and effects I have identified above. But she is left with the same subjective, potentially dismissible subjects: the fluctuations of emotional life, the embarrassments of eros, family and its entanglements, and so on. Since linguistic flourish has been ruled out, since she won't write poems in traditional forms, and since she won't indulge politics, history, or philosophy per se, she must find alternate ways of "objectifying" her poems. (Her irony is only one, relatively minor, way of achieving this.) The first way, I argue, is to put her simplified diction in the mouths of speakers whose dramatic mandates it seems not to suit. Next, she turns to mythic plots, like *The Odyssey*, which function as a counterpoint to her own life narrative and a means of investigating narrative itself—its claims, its distortions. Most recently, in her long poem "Prism," Glück has developed her long interest in didactic subgenres like riddle and parable, interspersing them with more conventional lyricism to write a nonnarrative, indeed "prismatic" autobiography.

Generic Speech

In the course of Glück's career, simple speech replaces what Mutlu Blasing calls "expressionist" speech. Blasing writes of Plath: "Unable to ascend or descend to a fluency 'above' or 'below' the scripts that assign her her words, [Plath] is arrested on the impossible ground of literary language, a middle ground of exile where she wanders on the stilts of iambs" (62). Glück will end up writing (in Blasing's terms) "below" such scripts—in an idiom marked by economy and expressive insufficiency; but she starts out very near where Plath finishes. In "Silverpoint," an early poem of Glück's, we get a painterly scene of a woman sunbathing:

> My sister, by the chiming kinks
> Of the Atlantic Ocean, takes in light.
> Beyond her, wreathed in algae, links on links
> Of breakers meet and disconnect, foam through bracelets
> Of seabirds. The wind sinks. She does not feel the change
> At once. It will take time. My sister,
> Stirring briefly to arrange
> Her towel, browns like a chicken, under fire.
>
> (*First Four* 16)

The poem, though far from Plath in tone and subject matter, is otherwise virtually a pastiche of Plathean techniques (and lines: Plath, in "Ariel," "foams / to wheat, a glitter of seas"): the scatter-shot rhymes, the stern enjambment ("links on links / Of break-ers," "bracelets / Of seabirds,") the verbs cut from the cloth of substantives or modifiers: "wreath," "foam," "brown." Elsewhere the volume is thick with Plathean images—oceans, onions, en-gines—that contribute to the book's atmosphere of borrowed flourish, borrowed pain.

The point is not to dwell on Glück's early borrowings (she was twenty-two when her first book was published) but rather to see, even within Glück's oeuvre, the kind of speech her own mature speech replaces. "Silverpoint" establishes, *via* Plath, a speaker whose expressive repertoire includes metaphor and simile, whose images are workshop-exact and "fresh," and whose voice oper-ates against and within the discipline of strict, and surprisingly regular, iambic rhythm. Like Lowell in *Life Studies* (a book to which this poem owes an additional debt) Glück achieves speak-erly mastery by phrase-by-phrase, line-by-line manipulation of form; her casualness seems hammered out of iron. Like Lowell and Plath before her, Glück stakes her claim on neologism and ingenuity of trope, aspects of what Lowell calls, in his sonnet "Robert Frost," "brilliant talk." Such talk presupposes, and often explicitly addresses, an auditor: not the aggregate "you" of Plath but rather, usually, a specific party, at times named.

When Glück turns to a new style, she abandons the adjective-rich "accurate" description of *Firstborn* in favor of a minimalism that acknowledges the limits of linguistic depiction. The ele-ments of the new style (a style Glück has since adapted and per-fected but never rejected) are audible in another sun-drenched descriptive poem, "Still Life":

Father has his arm around Tereze.
She squints. My thumb
is in my mouth: my fifth autumn.
Near the copper beech

> the spaniel dozes in the shadows.
> Not one of us does not avert his eyes.
> Across the lawn, in full sun, my mother
> stands behind her camera.
>
>   (*First Four* 73)

Only the barest descriptive resources are here employed: "objective" adjectives (a "copper" beech, my "fifth" autumn, "full" sun); simple verbs (only "dozes," the dog's action, conveys any affect at all); and an emblematic cast and location. That the poem is manifestly a "photograph" seems appropriate enough, given such a style, but the metaphor should be carefully parsed. Glück's "photographic" style is not the style Lowell describes in "Epilogue" and employs in *Day by Day*. There, the "photographic" means whatever is too candid or fleeting or incidental to register in a more deliberately artful style, indeed in Lowell's own earlier, more artful styles:

> sometimes everything I write
> with the threadbare art of my eye
> seems a snapshot,
> lurid, rapid, garish, grouped,
> heightened from life,
> yet paralyzed by fact.
>
>   (Lowell, *Collected Poems* 838)

Where the "snapshot" records "fact" (since its subjects move unselfconsciously through the world), the photographic portrait—the sort of photograph that interests Glück—tries (as much as possible given its medium) to erase fact: the family's ordinary comings and goings are frozen into conventionality, into a pose that is emblematic, but not documentary, of "family." The irony of any such portrait is that the conventionality of the family pose only heightens and offsets individual affect: the gloating and furtive and distracted looks that might disappear in an idealized portrait painting are here, in a portrait photograph, exaggerated. This "life" is anything but "still": "Not one of us does not avert his eyes." Of course the irony of the poem, and of the photograph, is also characteristic of Glück: the deadpan, by suppressing its own possibility of tonal flourish, is a better register of minute variation in the world. The thick, oily strokes of "Silverpoint" announce painterly mastery (and, in that case, borrowed inspiration); "Still Life" suppresses its own artfulness in order to chart the conventions according to which we compose the "natural."

As a metaphor for her poetics, then, Glück's photographic "Still Life" captures her interest in generic diction, as well as her belief that the personal life is irretrievably conventional, and most conventional precisely where it seems most personal. It does not, however, capture a third aspect of her poetics, and one that is equal in importance to the other two: namely, her interest in explicitly dramatic scenarios. In the mouth of the unnamed speaker of "Still Life," generic diction sounds deadpan, ironic, detached, as it often does in mature Glück; but unlike many of Glück's poems, "Still Life" seems largely unprovoked, lacking immediate psychological antecedents. Such unmarked lyric speech creates, Glück knows, "the illusion of stopped time"; the family must stand still both for the photograph and for the poem, and presumably for as long as the poem, or portrait, takes. Everyone acts conventionally in explicitly conventional moments like the one in "Still Life"; the proof of Glück's imaginative resourcefulness will come in her ability, instead, to apply "generic" language to emotionally specific (and dynamic) dilemmas and to find the conventional—to find the "Still Life"—at the heart of spontaneity.

To do so, Glück has to put her generic words in the mouths of speakers, and those speakers must address auditors with real claims (a husband, God, a son) on the speaker's emotional life. "It never occurred to me I wouldn't be a poet until I read Wallace Stevens," Glück has said, and in expressing a preference for the speech shapes of Eliot over the thought shapes of Stevens, Glück suggests the role of the "listener" in lyric poems: "I'd been reading Eliot. I had felt the presence essential to those poems. They're spoken in low tones, in whispers, to a companion or confessor; their strategies make of groping an aesthetic. They advance, they hesitate, they retreat: they announce *doubt* in language. The *cri de coeur* craves a listener, a single listener who becomes, by virtue of his absorption, Eliot's collaborator" (*Proofs* 114). This craving for a single listener is a craving if not for response at least for the acoustics of potential response, indeed of withheld response: These dramatic lyrics desire "counter-love," to borrow Frost's term, but seem bent on thwarting that desire. This strange effect of both inviting and foreclosing response is characteristic of Glück's dramatic poems. The response either does not come or, as in *Meadowlands*, comes, as a projection of the question, in a voice indistinct from the question. The irremediable solitariness-within-society of a Glück speaker, coupled with her generic diction, contributes to what critics have called her "otherworldly" tone. Glück's poems often imitate forms of explicit address—prayer, hymn, confession; in her book-length sequences *The Wild Iris* and *Meadowlands* she includes, within and between individual lyrics, the other voices who had, before, sat silent: the "husband" we have come to know by reference, along with the "son." But even there, where we hear Odysseus's rebuttal of Penelope's charges, the auditor (Odysseus) is never more or less than an aspect of the speaking voice, of the addressing voice (Penelope). The husband we hear in *Meadowlands* sounds, to our surprise (he is introduced in the fourth poem of the sequence) much like the Penelope to whom we have grown accustomed: so much like her that it, Odysseus' voice, must be marked off spatially within individual poems by indentation.

In establishing immediate stakes for generic diction, then, Glück must frame such diction as speech and, furthermore, as compelled speech. Like Browning (and unlike Wordsworth) she is interested in the things people say under adverse conditions for speech, such speech being more psychologically revealing than the speech that issues from self-composure. Glück wants her speakers to perform themselves into life under immediate emotional duress, in front of auditors with real, and often competing, claims; but she refuses Browning's aptness, his sense that personality, authentically rendered, ultimately acquits us all. She is drawn to one dramatic situation in particular—namely, the marital quarrel. She has written courtship poems, aubades, and poems of the marital quotidian as well, but the pitch of quarrel suits her desire to speak "urgently" better than any of those modes. No poet before Glück, however, has tried to render marital strife in generic language, and so in treating Glück's generic speech it is necessary to consider, however briefly, its antecedents. There is ample precedent, from Milton forward, for the exaggerated specificity of marital quarrel: the "mutual accusation" of book 9 of *Paradise Lost* finds Adam and Eve summoning all the available evidence in making their case, and doing so in some of the most beautiful poetry of *Paradise Lost*. Poets have tended to imagine marital quarrel as a theater of personality, where affect is heightened and strengthened, but Glück (virtually alone among poets) flattens and muffles heartbroken speech while still preserving what she calls its "urgency." In prelapsarian Eden Milton's lovers speak for the race and as the race; after the Fall they "take their solitary way," speaking as individuated persons and personalities. In *The Waste Land* Eliot figured quarrel as an exchange between the verbal and the oneiric, the explicitly and urgently "spoken" and the resignedly and bitterly "thought":

> "My nerves are bad to-night. Yes, bad. Stay with me.
> Speak to me. Why do you never speak? Speak.
> What are you thinking of? What thinking? Think."
>
> I think we are in rats' alley
> Where the dead men lost their bones.
>
> (Eliot 40)

The oneiric ("I think we are in rat's alley / Where the dead men lost their bones") answers the spoken as the communal answers the personal, as the imagistic answers the literal: Eliot's quarrel between man and wife is equally a quarrel between two ways of describing the horror of the immediate. The paranoid specificity of the wife's interrogation offsets the husband's dreamy, explicitly "poetic" cast of mind, and since that cast of mind presides over the whole of the poem, we sense, in these lines, that the generative conditions of the famously "impersonal" poem are in fact (as Randall Jarrell and others have remarked) deeply personal. In Frost's quarrel poems (of which "Home Burial" is a perfect example) and in Plath's and Lowell's poems following Frost, the grounds of quarrel are made explicit in the course of quarrel, where the highly affective and the deeply lyrical coincide. The wife in "Home Burial" finds new expressive reaches at the very moment her indictment of her husband (for his business-like burial of their dead son) lands most damningly:

> If you had feelings, you that dug
> With your own hand—how could you?—his little grave;
> I saw you from that very window there,
> Making the gravel leap and leap in air,
> Leap up, like that, like that, and land so lightly
> And roll back down the mound beside the hole.
> I thought, Who is that man? I don't know him.
>
> (Frost 66)

In her disgusted description of her husband's rhythmic shoveling, the wife finds the precise sonic shape ("Leap up, like that, like that") of the line's semantic content, mimicking his work with her talk. Description is here not so much foreclosed as heightened and strengthened by explicitly "poetic" means: Frost would never write a line so perfectly exemplary of his own theory that "sentence sounds" create, as he says in another poem, a "tone of meaning . . . without the words." Marital quarrel tends to provoke expressive specificity, then: we know, in "Home Burial," exactly the grounds of the quarrel, its setting (the poem transpires, famously, on the allegorically freighted entry staircase of a New England farmhouse), and the temperamental dispositions of its combatants. But Glück's quarrels are marked by a disdain for specificity, a tendency that makes their referential content difficult to excavate. Though Glück's quarreling lovers speak intelligibly to one another, they refuse to do so to us: referential specificity seems to have been refined out of their conversation, as though by pained repetition. Her lovers participate in a language game whose rules are never fully disclosed to us.

"Mock Orange" is a kind of tableau vivant of marital strife. The speaker is a woman making large gestures of refusal, saying outlandish things for effect. Perhaps she is refusing her husband sex; the two of them stand in a bedroom looking out on their yard. Even these basic details, however, are conjectural: descriptive detail is largely absent from the poem, which operates instead by the manipulation of a few, repeated generic elements. The title refers to the mock-orange coronets once worn by brides and announces that the poem will unfold not in the arena we might expect—the world of domestic realia—but rather in the idealized world of symbol and archetype. Likewise, the primary speech act of the poem (refusal) transpires under the sign of myth:

> It is not the moon, I tell you.
> It is these flowers
> lighting the yard.

The insistence ("I tell you") of the eerie correction indicates that we are beginning in medias res, after at least one round of negotiations has passed. The terms of the quarrel, in this second round, have been refined almost beyond recognizable shape: the husband, perhaps, has just blamed his wife's refusal on some immediate cause, where she has staked out, for her part, more abstract territory. In the second round, though, the terms shift to their idealized forms ("mood," perhaps, becomes "moon"; "marriage" becomes "flower," its visible symbol), forms that seem oddly inadequate to the tone of insistent and forceful correction. The poem continues, moving by analogy toward its emotive center:

> I hate them.
> I hate them as I hate sex,
> the man's mouth
> sealing my mouth, the man's
> paralyzing body—

> and the cry that always escapes,
> the low, humiliating
> premise of union—

The "as" allows the speaker to turn away from the window, as it were; the phenomenal world of the poem disappears under the powerful analogy "flowers are like sex," where sex, the secondary term, compels the poem's primary assertion: that "the cry that always escapes" is a "premise" (not, that is, a promise) of "union"— scripted, like everything else in the drama of conjugal love, and especially so for its purported spontaneity. The chiasmus of man/mouth/mouth/man expresses this notion with axiomatic concision. If the same thing happens every time, with absolute predictability, under a given set of circumstances, can it be considered authentic or spontaneous? The loveless orgasm is proof positive, for Glück, that our intimate lives are ruled by premises, not promises; no husband (or lover) is any more or less than the man at the moment the wife's self dissolves in inadvertent climax.

The poem's inward trajectory (yard to bed to mind) continues in the next stanza, where the terms "husband" and "wife" are again revised:

> In my mind tonight
> I hear the question and pursuing answer
> fused in one sound
> that mounts and mounts and then
> is split into the old selves,
> the tired antagonisms. Do you see?
> We were made fools of.
> And the scent of mock orange
> drifts through the window.

Glück learns from William Carlos Williams the trick of mimicking, in language, the cadences of sexual intercourse (what Nabokov called "the porno-grapple"); as in Williams's "Queen Anne's Lace," the climax of "Mock Orange" solves nothing and leads inexorably to disillusionment. Glück's insistent, monosyllabic iambs ("that mounts and mounts and then / is split") bring the poem into contact with one of its tonal and representational limits: such an expense of spirit leads to what passes for, at least tonally, insight ("Do you see? / We were made fools of.") And since "mock orange" (like the apple in Genesis) ends up representing both the fact of difference ("the old selves, / the tired antagonisms") and the knowledge of difference ("Do you see? / We were made fools of") "rest" is impossible; the poem ends not on its penultimate note of resignation but with a rhythmically insistent quatrain:

How can I rest?
How can I be content
when there is still
that odor in the world?
    (*First Four* 155)

The ten perfect iambic feet suggest, at some distance, an "unwritten" pentameter couplet; but in practical terms the sudden metrical regularity forces us to put our emphasis squarely on the repeated word "can"—implying, of course, that in the white space between stanzas, the "you" has issued his poorly considered ("rest," "be content") imperatives.

"Mock Orange" is a poem that moves forward by insistent repetition ("It is not . . . it is," "I hate . . . I hate," "man's mouth . . . my mouth, "How can I . . . How can I . . ."), an effect that (coupled with the poem's strong rhythmic patterning) gives the impression of necessitated, unrehearsed speech, speech unfolding in relation to an immediate goad. Such rhythmic and rhetorical insistence is odd, though, in a poem so resistant to substantive specificity. We tend to think of "impassioned speech," in Glück's phrase, as expressive of the individuated, the nearly irretrievable elements in emotional life; "impassioned" speech, at least where lyric has represented it, expresses the specificities of the speaker's emotional dilemma. Frost's lovers (again "Home Burial " is my example), even where specific substantives elude them, still find "tones of meaning"—specific contours of speech ("Leap up, like that, like that") within the necessities of the pentameter line. Glück's speakers cannot find such pitches of speech; as I suggest above, they speak as though one round of talk has passed, as though, in speaking, they've grown tired from speaking. Their stories come to seem, even to them, absurdly scripted, coded in a DNA suddenly clearly legible. These stories, because their essence is interchangeability, cannot be "done" accurately unless they recognize the script behind spontaneity, a script Glück comes to represent by means of myth.

"Personal Matters": Meadowlands

Any poet interested in the expressive use of voices not-necessarily-hers will turn, at some point in her career, to voices necessarily-not-hers. Where "Mock Orange" suggested, but refused to name outright, its participation in the Genesis myth, *Meadowlands* explicitly acknowledges myth—Homer's *Odyssey.* "My work," Glück has said, "has always been marked by a disregard for the circumstantial, except insofar as it could be transformed into paradigm." Poets who write within myth do so, usually, to efface the marks of "personality" within a traditional frame: the poet adopting a mythic persona chooses, to one degree or another, anonymity over a fixed, specific identity. Glück finds human conduct highly conventionalized, as I have argued, and most so where it seems most deeply personal. But mythic material is of further use to Glück, as Bonnie Costello has said, as an "alternative standard of measurement" ("Trustworthy Speakers" 15), a grid against which the fluctuations of the self can be plotted.

The distinction between "self" and "mask" is founded on assumptions I do not wish to embrace: suffice it to say that any lyric performance is a mask if the self prior to artifactual shaping is taken to be the coherent and authentic one. But a poet interested in the autobiographical self, as Glück inarguably is, does something counter to her explicit purpose in assuming a persona; and the more conventional the persona—the more public the property, so to speak—the further the poet travels from the narrow provinces of private and autobiographical material. The use of masks, of course, was among the strategies of high modernism; but Glück's use of masks is different from, say, Yeats's, both in theory and in practice. Yeats is not, to the same degree as Glück, interested in documenting the autobiographical self. Yeats tends to see even the most personal material under the sign of legend or symbol; his "facts" tend to emblematic of spirit, his characters (even those with recognizable personal significance) exemplary of the "casual comedy" of human life. Yeats is interested in the flamboyance and exuberance of personality but not in the documentation of lived life per se. He uses masks, therefore, not so much to analogize the lived self as to transform (sometimes, famously, by negation) the "person seated at the breakfast table" into viable aesthetic form: "A poet writes always of his personal life, in his finest work out of its tragedy, remorse, lost love, or mere loneliness; he never speaks directly as to someone at the breakfast table, there is always a phantasmagoria" (Yeats, *Essays* 509). Since for Yeats all poetic performance involves the construction of a "phantasmagoria," the poet who chooses to write in a persona does so in confirmation of the primary act of lyric writing. But by the time Glück writes her Odyssean book *Meadowlands*, a set of conventions for "speaking directly" have been developed: poets of Glück's generation (as I have said) have available to them an "authentic" or "sincere" style. The person "at the breakfast table," like so many other versions of the ordinary, appears and disappears from the art of any given era with the discovery and loss of conventions that make such "ordinariness" aesthetically available, but no style of earlier lyric ever found such convincing means of presenting the ordinary life as did the confessionalism of Glück's immediate predecessors.

Glück's choice of mythological personae, then, must be understood as a strategy not of erasing the autobiographical self, or of transforming it into Yeatsian exuberance, but rather as a means of presenting it in other, analogous terms. Costello argues that, with *Meadowlands*, Glück discovers "trustworthy" speakers, possibly for the first time in her career—speakers, that is, who not only mean what they say but whose account of things would hold up to external corroboration. The poet is able to do so, according to Costello, because of the "distancing devices" inherent in the contemporary employment of myth generally and Glück's use of the *Odyssey* specifically. Such devices "do not erase the self,"

Costello argues but, rather, "they create perspective that clarifies sight, as when we step back to see a detail of a painting in terms of the whole" ("Trustworthy Speakers" 6). Glück had of course sought such perspective before, in other poems, playing characters from a variety of sources—Eve, Achilles, God, Gretel. In *The Wild Iris* she takes the voices—wonderfully petulant or hopeful or snide—of flowers. But *The Odyssey* serves a special purpose for Glück, since, while it presents the consciousness of Penelope as central, it has within it means of counterbalancing her claims. Here again is Costello: "There is something Greek, and fatalistic, about the encounters between the figures in this story. Each figure is rooted in an immovable passion, but the collision of these passions creates drama ... [not merely a psychomachia]" ("Trustworthy Speakers" 8). Characters in *Meadowlands* need not be self-divided, since their world is so clearly portioned out. Circe (who, like Penelope, addresses Odysseus) creates a kind of visible border of Penelope's woe; the adolescent Telemachus demarcates the entire drama, with his wry, deflationary insights. The absurdly circumscribed world of *The Odyssey*, by its very circumscription, allows each figure to speak confidently about her dilemma, the narrowed parameters of speech being visible to every character at every moment.

Meadowlands is what Helen Vendler has named (referring to Robert Lowell) a "transparent myth" (*Part* 144)—a myth whose selective employment (the structure of the *Odyssey* but not its tone, *nostos* but not Troy) forces us to read it as an allegorized autobiography. In such a scheme, Penelope "is" Louise Glück in a way that Glück's earlier, disembodied speakers—the speaker of "Mock Orange" is a perfect example—were not. We weren't provoked by "Mock Orange" to wonder about the real Glück's real marriage, as indeed we do reading *Meadowlands*. This "autobiography effect" of *Meadowlands* is present even in its title, with its simultaneous admission of both the mythological and the contemporary. The book's riskiest moment, perhaps, comes when (late in the sequence, as a kind of afterthought) it acknowledges that it shares its name with the New Jersey football stadium home to—who else?—the Giants. "Kings among men," the husband figure asserts; while, in response, the wife figure asks "So what king fired Simms?" "Meadowlands 3" is exactly the kind of poem that makes criticism ashamed of itself; it sounds like overstatement, given a poem so light on its mythological feet, to listen for the Olympian echoes—to read famously hapless Quarterback Phil Simms as a Cyclopean "giant" and the Giants general manager as, perhaps, an eternally shamed Poseidon. Conversely, Ulysses, unlike the Ulysses figure of *Meadowlands*, did not arrive in Troy "suntanned from his time away, wanting / his grilled chicken" (3); but such moments in Glück force us to read Ulysses and Penelope—the authorized protagonists of the sequence—under the sign of the contemporary, perhaps (from the insistent, irrational specificity of the details) as autobiography.

The relentless ordinariness of "grilled chicken"—like the ordinariness of the Giants' football stadium—establishes one pole of *Meadowlands*, a kind of counterpoint to the innate gravitas of Homeric epic. Though we might explain such "circumstantial" details as merely ironic, merely deflationary, they are in fact of far greater importance. More often than ever before in Glück's work, the speakers of *Meadowlands* must account for, and understand themselves in light of, the ordinary. Where Glück's previous speakers inhabit the world of what Glück calls "paradigm," Penelope finds herself foundering at the limits of paradigm, where comical "details" obsess the self. In "Midnight" she finds herself "weeping in the dark garage":

> Speak to me, aching heart: what
> ridiculous errand are you inventing for yourself
> weeping in the dark garage
> with your sack of garbage: it is not your job
> to take out the garbage, it is your job
> to empty the dishwasher.
> (*Meadowlands* 26)

The passage turns on the difference between an "errand" (with its muted Spenserian echoes) and a "job"—the former being freighted with significance, the latter being rote, memorized, an evasion of significance. Manic repetition (garage/garbage/ garbage) parodies the old, lost world of easy domestic routine, but it is also the way one talks to steady the heart. The Odyssean "standard of measurement," to use Costello's helpful term, for such a scene is perhaps Penelope's exaggerated devotion and its material form, her weaving. And in place of Penelope's patience, her decorum, we have self-rebuke and complex, many-faceted irony, irony that lampoons both the other (a husband who assigns chores) and the self (a wife who accepts them).

It is important to the book's overall seriousness, then, that it not take a uniformly ironic stance in relation to its own mythic claims, not see the contemporary marriage as merely fallen, banal, or "mock epic" in its reality. For Glück, marital life not only suggests the mythic—suggests an analogous structure—but in fact creates or coins "mythic" structures of its own. It is the case not only that "suntan" and "grilled chicken" are antimythic elements, fallen versions of the Odyssean detail (perhaps of Odysseus's famous scar, which reveals his identity in Ithaca) but that such details take on, in their psychic import and within the economy of a marriage, mythic functions. The easy commerce between mythic material and circumstantial material is a result of this original and inevitable conflation of the two. The marriage— "marriage"—includes myth; myth is both its cause and its natural result. Thus the "bickering" of swans comes to constitute song:

> On the muddy water
> they bickered awhile, in the fading light,
> until the bickering grew
> slowly abstract, becoming
> part of their song
> after a little longer.
>
> (*Meadowlands* 52)

The substitution of mythic discourse for marital conversation, then, is easily enough accomplished: but such a substitution shocks in its wide-ranging appropriateness, so that each

successful poem—each substitution of the mythic for the personal that works—both saddens and hardens the lyric speaker.
Emotive engagement, for Glück as for Yeats, ends in "wisdom";
but wisdom is ever sighing for its previous form, desire. Here is
the final stanza of "Heart's Desire," the last poem of *Meadowlands*:

> If you can hear the music
> you can imagine the party.
> I have it all planned: first
> violent love, then
> sweetness. First *Norma*
> then maybe the Lights will play.
> > (*Meadowlands* 60)

That inevitable sweetness, of course, indicts the violent love it
sprang from; consciousness of myth is consciousness of the final
form any event will take, plotting the moment's event in a narrative line. It could be argued, further, that the mythic is always
ordering our emotional lives—that the conscious and deliberate
substitution of Homer for the personal is in fact a substitution of
Homer for some other myth—for Freud, perhaps, or for the version of Sophocles or of Aeschylus that Freud sponsored. And,
in that we live out certain paradigms established in childhood
(itself a myth, but one believed by many poets and certainly by
Glück), we are all living within the mythic. "We fill pre-existing
forms," says Frank Bidart, "and when we fill them change them
and are changed" (*Desire*). Or, as Glück says: "We look at the
world once, in childhood. The rest is memory" (*Meadowlands*
23–24).

The "transparency" of *Meadowlands* depends, then, on the
incorporation of the circumstantial into Homeric paradigms, and
the inclusion of such realia is a new technique for Glück. The
book is, as Costello says in "Trustworthy Speakers," the most
"social" of Glück's volumes, the most interested in what men
and women say to one another in recognizable domestic scenes.
This interest is apparent in the several colloquies that punctuate

the book, where voice is marked as explicitly "spoken" and, what's more, spoken in dialogue. It is as though the implied interlocutor of "Mock Orange" were suddenly given words. "Anniversary" is short enough to quote in full:

> I said you could snuggle. That doesn't mean
> your cold feet all over my dick.
>
> Someone should teach you how to act in bed.
> What I think is you should
> keep your extremities to yourself.
>
> Look what you did—
> you made the cat move.
>
> But I didn't want your hand there.
> I wanted your hand here.
> You should pay attention to my feet.
> You should picture them
> the next time you see a hot fifteen year old.
> Because there's a lot more where those feet come from.
>
> (*Meadowlands* 21)

As in "Mock Orange" we know the setting (bed) and the dramatis personae (man and wife, or perhaps man, wife, and cat) but not the precise stakes of the argument. The difficulty of uncovering the "real" form of this verbal form is suggested, perhaps, by the unlikely position ("feet" on "dick"?) the lovers take: no conjugal bed ever looked quite like this one. And the liminal position of "snuggling"—implying, that is, something other than and less than intercourse—is confirmed by the presence of the cat: how difficult it is, perhaps, to "snuggle" deliberately without things going one way or another. The poem, then, is about "how to act in bed"—how to act naturally after the world has taken on regulation and, analogously, how to "act naturally" in the deliberate space of a poem. As such, "naturalness" is acknowledged as a fiction, and the question of where one's body is precisely, vis-à-vis the other, becomes *the* question for the couple.

One's body, but also one's voice. In "Ithaca" Glück has Penelope say of Odysseus:

> He was two people.
> He was the body and voice, the easy
> magnetism of a living man, and then
> the unfolding dream or image
> shaped by the woman working the loom,
> sitting there in a hall filled
> with literal-minded men.
>
> (*Meadowlands* 12)

The "body and voice" that fills the hall is different in kind, Glück thinks, from the "unfolding dream or image" ("unfolding," that is, even in the absolute present of this poem); voices in a poem emerge, always, from the distorted acoustics of a single consciousness, and a poem that acknowledges the weight and drag of the voice's passage trumps a realistic presentation of speech. In this bed, furthermore, man and woman speak alike: Glück is at pains to slow down our attribution of voice to any continuous and realistic "character." Of course the voice we hear first belongs to the man, but are we to take the stanza break as a shift of speaker? The second stanza ("Someone should . . .") could function either in response to the first or in elaboration of it; "extremities" is tonally precise (and precisely nasty) but could refer either to the "feet" or the "dick." We find, eventually, that the poem has means of marking off speech—the responsorial is indented, indicating that the poem is more or less evenly divided between husband and wife—but we find it in spite of the poem's other effects, and in relation to them. The necessity of indentation—of providing a spatial cue, outside of the poem's manifest performance (and difficult, one would think, to replicate vocally)—confesses precisely how undifferentiated the voices are.

The obfuscation of gender at a point when ordinary speech is most thoroughly gendered; the flattening of affect at a highly affective moment; the refusal to grant special pardon to one "side" of a marital quarrel or another: all of these aspects of

"Anniversary" are typical of Glück's dialogue poems. As such they indicate a skepticism, perhaps even a pessimism, over lyric poetry's chances of representing authetic and sincere speech. Such a project for speech implies a theory of the self from which speech issues, a theory I will explain more fully later in this chapter. But such skepticism involves another strategy of presentation, a strategy that the very structure of dialogue suggests: namely, the use of narrative to unsteady momentary and static lyric events. No speaker in *Meadowlands* is without her counterspeaker; the primary lyric speaker of the poem is split into several "interests" that all, nevertheless, speak in the same voice. Similarly, Glück uses myth to disarm the singularity and self-sufficiency of lyric image making: her images, in *Meadowlands,* tend to be not static but dynamic. Glück will often attend to those transitional temporal states with perceptual consequences, especially to dusk and dawn, fall and spring. Attention to such states disarms description (the dearth of adjectives in a Glück poem suggests their low status in her poetics) since, in the time description takes, the world revises itself. Such revision is a crisis for the signifier; the problem of representing "impassive process" becomes one of *Meadowlands'* central thematic concerns. In "Quiet Evening" Penelope praises "the quiet evenings in summer, the sky still light at this hour"; a few poems later, in "Departure," she addresses her lover:

> The night isn't dark; the world is dark.
> Stay with me a little longer.
> > (*Meadowlands* 10)

Lyric speech takes place against the threat of abandonment, as the poem delays its auditor's eventual leave-taking. Glück's characters are always expecting simple temporal forms to bear emotional content, as in "Parable of the King":

> The great king looking ahead
> saw not fate but simply
> dawn glittering over
> the unknown island.
> > (*Meadowlands* 8)

Such moments are common throughout Glück's poems (there are dozens of poems with titles like "Aubade" and "Nocturne" as well as several "Evenings" and "Mornings") but her interest in such states is crucial to understanding her choice of the *Odyssey* in *Meadowlands*. The structure of the Odyssey—its special way of thematizing narrative itself, and its richness as a metaphor for epistemology (explored by Stevens among others) lends special emphasis to Glück's interest in such transitional states. Just as Glück's uniformity of tone (discussed above) suggests doubt about the very prospect that a lyric poem could present, within its narrow boundaries, a fully realized and independent speaker, such skepticism is confirmed by the structural properties of the Odyssey. Just as each player in the *Odyssey* moves, as a kind of chess piece, only in reaction to the last move made, so each new "voice" in *Meadowlands* seems to have memorized its next, its appropriate, move. Even the outbursts in *Meadowlands* are deadpan. This strange collaborative sigh—each speaker saying and doing his part, as though at the end of a long, uninspired run—reflects one of the book's profoundest themes: the difficult necessity of making a single object capable of representing the passing of time. The temporal paradox is present, of course, in Glück's choice to import a narrative form—written myth—into lyric but is even more so in her obvious desire to import the narrativeness of such a narrative form. The Horatian imperative that epic should begin in medias res is honored, though now, since the existence of a narrative poem called The *Odyssey* necessitates a new point of origin (since Homer is now, to quote Stevens, "part of the *res*"), we begin with Penelope at her loom, late in the story, nearly in the *nostos*. The problem of writing narrative within lyric is explicitly addressed at several points, notably at the close of "Moonless Night":

> Such a mistake to want
> clarity above all things. What's
> a single night, especially
> one like this, now so close to ending?
> On the other side, there could be anything,

all the joy in the world, the stars fading,
the streetlight becoming a bus stop.

(*Meadowlands* 9)

Replace the word "night" with the word "poem" and you have a neat declaration on the limits of lyric representation, within which even the narrative drive to turn the page for more is thwarted ("On the other side, there could be anything . . .") How do we then, in poems of the heightened moment, represent the passing of such moments?

At times Glück's *Odyssey* seems, then, to be (as it is for Stevens) an elaborate metaphor for perception; though as in Stevens perception is itself usually a metaphor for emotional states of becoming and dissolving. Odysseus's return is anything long sought coming into focus; and so anything long sought coming into focus is Odysseus's return. But arrival—as both Stevens and Glück know—is the death of process, and all the moral arguments are, again for both Stevens and Glück, on the side of process. Arrival, at least structurally, mirrors death; deferral, in contrast, mirrors life. Making your book of poems a long narrative sequence solves one very real problem of particularity, by forcing every image in a given poem to stand up to the chance of its later, inevitable revision: within the book there are several sub-sequences that provide a latest version of an earlier figure or event. As in a conventional narrative—as in Homer—events of whatever kind wait on subsequent events: we see the neighbors, the cat, the grilled chicken several times and must reorient ourselves to them with each new occurrence.

Antinarrative Autobiography: "Prism"

The *Odyssey* is a narrative poem that allegorizes narrative: the break that narrative establishes with "real" time is figured by the rape of Helen; the conditions of narrative time are spatialized and given psychological depth by the stations—Troy, the islands—Odysseus must visit; Ithaca and Penelope are the always-present reconciliation that narrative tends toward but delays. The *Odyssey*, in imbuing any present moment with expectation, in establishing all action in time as delay, gives the lie to any moment's mere momentariness.

In writing within Homer, Glück is renewing a classic dilemma for lyric, what Sharon Cameron calls "the contradiction between social and personal time." Cameron argues: "If a poem denies the centrality of beginnings and ends, if it fails to concern itself with the accumulated sequence of history, it must push its way into the dimensions of the moment, pry apart its walls and reveal the discovered space there to be as complex as the long corridors of historical and narrative time" (230). As a writer of novella-like poetic sequences (and as a devoted reader of mystery novels) Glück's stance is vexed attraction, rather than an aversion, to narrative. For her "personal time" and "social time" are too complexly braided to be so easily distinguished. For the reasons I have described above, Glück abhors unselfconscious narrative, just as she abhors any sense of the personal that ignores its paradigmatic frame. Her impulse is, rather, to explain the personal by means of acknowledging, even somewhat starkly, the frame. With narrative, too, Glück finds that writing within structures viably requires making them manifest. (But making them manifest would seem to demystify them and perhaps, therefore, to invalidate them emotionally.)

And so with her remarkable autobiographical poem "Prism," whose title indicates a structure of alternating "faces," nonlinear in sequence, un- or loosely chronological, with an impressionistic, rather than strictly causal, logic of development. The poem is in twenty sections, no one section longer than twenty-one lines and many sections only a very few lines. Picture a spherical prism suspended from a chain, rotating on its axis and, as it does so, revealing new faces, projecting new wavelengths. Like Stevens's "Planet on the Table" it is manifestly a miniature world that replaces the world. Appropriately, therefore, it begins with an acknowledgment, equal parts repudiation and embrace, of "the world":

> Who can say what the world is? The world
> is in flux, therefore
> unreadable, the winds shifting,
> the great plates invisibly shifting and changing—

The poem begins by foreclosing one possible path, the path of synoptic, transcendent vision. For the "unreadable" world it will substitute a "readable" one, namely, itself. As this poem builds itself, it builds its world. But because it is a prism, it functions by fragmenting existing reality into "manageable" portions. In section 2, it finds a level, barren place and begins, with the few tools lying around, "constructing" its shelter:

> Dirt. Fragments
> of blistered rock. On which
> the exposed heart constructs
> a house, memory; the gardens
> manageable, small in scale, the beds
> damp at the sea's edge—

This small stay against exposure is one of many attempts in the poem to master the "unreadable" world by portioning it out into its constituent parts. In place of the world that offers unmediated, and therefore imperiling, reality ("exposure") it "constructs" a world, phrase by phrase, unreal though manageable. The poem counterpoints its own linguistic construction with the failed constructions of others. Glück's sister's erotic "formula" ("When you fall in love . . . it's like being struck by lightning") fails because it "repeats exactly" their mother's formula and "what we were looking at in the adults // were the effects not of lightning / but of the electric chair." Glück's own self-description in a later section fails for the same reasons:

> When I was a child, I suffered from insomnia.
> Summer nights, my parents permitted me to sit by the lake;
> I took the dog for company.
> Did I say "suffered"? That was my parents' way of explaining
> tastes that seemed to them
> inexplicable: better "suffered" than "preferred to live with the dog."

The function of these linguistic artifacts, formulas, riddles, codes, and other reiterated descriptions is to hypostasize essentially dynamic, shifting phenomena. These are the illegitimate forms of the poem's own method of mastery—self-ennobling or self-inoculating linguistic artifacts from which Glück's preferred variety of artifact, lyric poetry, must distinguish itself.

What do we do when faced with the inscrutable? We may reduce it to a code, translatable into another, more familiar code ("The word [marry] was a code, mysterious, like the Rosetta stone"). Or develop crude means of orientation, like road signs or signposts or crude epistemological road signs and signposts like riddles. Riddles are especially important in "Prism," adding to its ambience of concealed or obscured meaning. (In this respect alone it recalls Frost's poem "Directive" and its suggestion that—as in a quest—memory is the successful recovery, through time, of precious and imperiled objects.)

Riddle:
Why was my mother happy?

Answer:
She married my father.

The attraction of riddles is in their structure of suspended certitude, as the nearby and actual is made strange by fresh description. Riddles are not questions without answers but, rather, questions whose answers are hidden in plain sight. The deliberate mystification of what is plainly obvious is consistent with this poem's remembered world, where the sense of being involved in a mystery means everything, no matter how slight, might be a clue. Mysteries have this advantage over other kinds of narratives, that they sharpen perception into scrutiny.

But what is a remembered mystery? A remembered riddle? As structures of sharpened expectation, both mysteries and riddles create a strong future tense. Temporary deprivation will be replaced, in both cases, by satiety. (The pleasure of riddles and mysteries arises from the desire for temporary—"manageable," to borrow Glück's word—deprivation.) But down the long corridor of remembered time, "Prism" sights its answers and its questions simultaneously. The riddles have their solutions yoked to them, the mysteries, large and small, are solved (or at least settled). It is this notion, of remembered palpable futurity, a self tensed for coming crisis recalled long after the crisis has been suffered, that most distinguishes "Prism." This mode opposes the false naïveté of many poems about childhood, where subsequent knowledge must be disavowed, erased, in favor of perceptual and idiomatic fidelity to the child's world. (Bishop's marvelous, overexposed poems about childhood, with their whitewashing of affect and image, would be an example.) A walk by the boat basin becomes, in "Prism," an immensely subtle blocking out of one's selves in relation to one another, within time:

> Darkness. Silence that annulled mortality.
> The tethered boats rising and falling.
> When the moon was full, I could sometimes read the girls' names
> painted to the sides of the boats:
> *Ruth Ann, Sweet Izzy, Peggy My Darling—*
>
> They were going nowhere, those girls.
> There was nothing to be learned from them.

The "rising and falling" of the boats, discernible only within a scene otherwise darkened and silenced, will later (in the poem and in the life) become the "breathing" of lovers in a darkened room. Within the silence and darkness of the scene, something additional can be made out: internal, slight variety, so that "when the moon was full I could sometimes"—only sometimes, within the existing "sometimes" when the moon was full—"read." What we read that Glück "reads" on those moonlit nights is the consequentiality, from the point of view of the future, of present things (the boats that will come to mean breathing, the girls' names from which "there was nothing to be learned"). It is the most natural thing in the world, of course, to project oneself into the future perfect: often we say of things, "that will have been nothing" or "that will have been something." In this poem the additional overlay of actual recollection adds tremendous, almost eerie poignancy to these moments of forecasted or imagined recollection.

This poem must, therefore, invent a readable world, then read it. It must find a language for memory that is neither amusement nor anodyne but one that nevertheless provides shelter for the exposed heart. Its prismatic structure (avoiding narrative causation) is one method; its strict monitoring of language, its own and others', is another; its self-consciousness as an artifact (the poem is named "Prism," not "Childhood") is a third. Its habit of placing itself feeling fully within overlapping time frames, being at once recollective and prospective *and* recollective-prospective is for me its most profound method. These strategies are "distancing devices," to use Costello's helpful term, but (as with her use of Homer) since they function as checks on sentiment they also make sentiment possible. Scenes that in another poet's hands might seem photogenic, angled for delicacy, seem, in "Prism," hard-won. Cameron's "personal time" has been retrieved, in these scenes, since it exists only as one prismatic face among many:

> The room was quiet.
> That is, the room was quiet, but the lovers were breathing.
>
> In the same way, the night was dark.
> It was dark, but the stars shone.
>
> The man in bed was one of several men
> to whom I gave my heart. The gift of the self,
> that is without limit.
> Without limit, though it recurs.

In addition to the temporal dislocations of "Prism" and owing to them, there is also in this poem a kind of deliberate blunting of identity. Personal reminiscence (the dog, the boats), though vivid, is subordinated to forms of anonymity. What one finds in childhood is not some essential ore of person but, rather, an alloy of person forged by forces (familial, social, historical) outside oneself. The self is clearest, in "Prism," at moments when one is fiercely resisting others' descriptions of it ("our mother's formula," "suffered"), blurriest when left to one's own descriptive resources. We can say with great certainty what we are not, but the ground-note of self-description is doubt. Anonymity is not, here, to be construed solely negatively. The loss of self is ecstasy as often as it is endangerment.

For Glück's mother, speaking to her daughters, "There is no one like you father"; for Glück, "The man in bed was one of several men // to whom I gave my heart:

> I'm in a bed. This man and I,
> we are suspended in the strange calm
> sex often induces. Most sex induces.
> Longing, what is that? Desire, what is that?
> In the window, constellations of summer.
> Once, I could name them

The man, the constellations, the "I"—each of these elements is abstracted, rather comfortingly, into paradigm. "I could name them, I had names for them," Glück will say, a little later in the poem: "Two different things." Different because the act of naming something bestows identity on it, inflexible and permanent, whereas having a name for something simply orients us to it. The one gives essence, the other establishes relation. And when the poem ends, it ends with another loss of orientation, as the unnamed man in bed becomes, in the dawn light, "the stranger":

> A night in summer. Sounds of a summer storm.
> The great plates invisibly shifting and changing—
>
> And in the dark room, the lovers sleeping in each other's arms.
>
> We are, each of us, the one who wakens first,
> who stirs first and sees, there in the first dawn,
> the stranger.
>
> > (*Averno* 21 ff.)

In this poem where every relation is named (master, enemy, sister, father, mother, dog) and where identity is relational, the name "stranger" indicates a sudden vertigo within relation, a moment when, since the position of the other is so radically unfixed, one's own position becomes so. This loss of self is the nightmare form of the earlier, quite pleasant forms of anonymity, and a poem that had invoked "strange calm" ends where it began, in panic. The poem finished, the world resumes in its old, frightening, unreadable way.

Conclusion: Autobiography and the Language School

Retrospective Autobiography in Howe and Silliman

American poets can no longer say of themselves, as Gerard Manley Hopkins said so movingly, "I taste self but at one tankard, that of my own being." Selfhood now seems to be the most obviously constructed of ideas, despite—and because—it has long seemed the most natural thing in the world. There is no longer any intellectually credible way, it seems, of theorizing interiority as a pastoral refuge from the annihilations of culture. Even our nature poetry (I am thinking of Ammons) is antipastoral unless (again, in Ammons) it finds some place absurdly small or distant (humanly uninhabitable, except by the imagination) to inhabit. Language poets disavow referential language as coercive in itself. The prestige of poetry would seem to have been imperiled by its swerving too near the subject matter of novels and plays and, now, memoirs and talk shows. The culture at large has become, it seems, a culture of theatrical candor, while poetry—serious, ambitious, self-conscious poetry—has drunk from every tankard but the self.

Yet a surprising feature of experimental American poetries in the past several years has been their interest in autobiography as a concept. Several of the most important Language and post-Language writers have produced works that we might call in some sense "autobiographical": Lyn Hejinian's *My Life*, Fanny Howe's *The Wedding Dress*, Susan Howe's *Pierce-Arrow* and *Frame Structures*, Ron Silliman's *Under Albany*, as well as shorter works by Michael Palmer and Devin Johnston. These "autobiographical" projects by poets of the Language school and Language-influenced younger poets (poets of the so-called post-avant-garde) bear little resemblance, of course, to conventional autobiography. But it is important to note that the idea of casting one's poetics in terms of lived life is suddenly attractive to poets whose central tenets included not merely the rejection of life as a basis for art (indeed of the very terms "life" and "art") but, further, the rejection of any subject matter for poetry outside of language itself. What Marjorie Perloff, herself the author of a recent memoir, has called the "coming of age" of the Language school has often been simultaneously an arrival at autobiography. Silliman's "Albany"—a seminal Language text—was, as Perloff has written, "always already autobiographical" ("Language" 422).

It is tempting to see this autobiographical turn as a sign of how narrow and unsustainable were the principles of the Language school all along. Confirming Oren Izenberg's statement that "Language poets have tended . . . to misdescribe some of the most serious and interesting implications of their own practice" (133), when we look at its founding documents, we find statements so naive as to seem, twenty years after the fact, almost silly. Let us take one very famous example, Lyn Hejinian's statement about integrated subjectivity, later quoted by Perloff: "The 'personal' is already a plural condition. Perhaps one feels that it is located somewhere within, somewhere inside the body—in the stomach? the chest? the genitals? the throat? the head? One can look for it and already one is not oneself, one is several, incomplete, and subject to dispersal" (Hejinian 170). What this statement rather strangely overlooks is the possibility of the act of writing itself acting as proof against dispersal. Poetic performance has always taken as its occasion moments of self-dispersal, self-disintegration, vertigo. The very premise of a lyric self depends, I would argue, on the feeling of drift, flight, and distraction in persons. Romantic subjectivity might well be located in an interior, stable and secure, but surely it is only mined by unstable and even improvisatory systems like "the imagination" and by poetic language. Saying it exists prior to the poem is just a way of describing what finding it feels like. The integrated self is a linguistic construct, a thing made out of language, and like all such constructs it starts to age and wear as soon as it is finished. Acts of writing make the self they find.

The above statements, though meant to disprove Hejinian's assumptions about person, nevertheless pretty fairly summarize the recent work by some central figures of Hejinian's Language school and its affiliates. Silliman's and Howe's works are particularly interesting for being explicitly retrospective, a stance that would seem, based on their poetics, empty or even impossible. (There is no habit of contemporary poetry more ingrained than the use of the present tense to signal the simultaneity of writing acts and experience.) Surprisingly for poets so committed to the interrogation of conventional subjectivity, these works act as though a stable I-subject and a stable me-object were possible, even inevitable. The sense of a self as durable and consistent across time would seem to have been invalidated by Howe's and Silliman's earlier work.

Perloff very briefly compares Susan Howe's *Frame Structures* to Robert Lowell's work and particularly to his prose memoir "91 Revere Street." The point is worth elaborating here. Howe shares with Lowell her Brahmin heritage and a rigorous interest in the capacity of lyric to represent historical subjects. (Both Lowell and Howe think of lyric as resistant to historical material; otherwise their projects would be meaningless.) For both poets, the historical dimensions of the self are literally traceable, verifiable through time. What constitutes self for Lowell and Howe cannot help but include elements of civic, local, and national history. For both, the extension of self into ancestral experiences and acts is an occasion demanding lyric intervention. Lowell's "confessionalism," from his early poems forward, sought expiation not primarily for his own misdeeds but for those of his ancestors. Howe has twice (in *Pierce-Arrow* and in *The Midnight*) quoted Emerson's remark that "every man is a quotation from all his ancestors."

It is that word "quotation" that Howe finds most seductive in Emerson's formulation, for her style is often elaborately knitted from documents. Like Lowell, her historical imagination is engaged by objects (heirlooms especially) and documents: Howe's poetry is documentary in this literal sense. Her most ambitious work is archival in fact and manner: both *Pierce-Arrow*, nominally a poem, and *My Emily Dickinson*, nominally a work of literary criticism, quote at length from archival documents. Following the American Pragmatists she reveres and whom her work everywhere engages, Howe is interested in the relational energy released by textual adjacency: original lines of her own often jostle with these archival documents, some of them reproduced in their original typescript and manuscript forms within text of Howe's poems. The effect of reading a poem by Howe is to have upset every expectation of textual, even graphic, continuity, to a degree beyond even Pound's or Gertrude Stein's modernist dislocations.

These two concerns—a Lowell-like concern with the historicity of private selves, and a Stein-like or Pound-like concern with textual dislocation—produce Howe's distinctive style, a style deepened by deliberate acts of revision across time. In retrospect, Howe's poems seem to her symptomatic of, documentary of, the private self they seemed originally to reject. For a poet who finds herself plotted historically, who wakes to history at the same moment that she wakes to privacy, poems are themselves historical—or, more precisely, archival—documents. And so Howe's earliest poems, nearly forensic in their detachment from "autobiography" and its obsessions, have been collected under the title *Frame Structures*—itself a reference to New England's architectural heritage—with a new, autobiographical preface.

This preface suggests that Howe's early poems be read as symptoms of autobiography.

As her title indicates, Howe's poems from the period are bare minima, unadorned, built according to a radical primitivism of style. But the word "frame" also implies the frame around a painting, and indeed Howe began as a visual artist before she turned to writing poems. This double sense of "frame"—implying artlessness and functionality in the first case, and self-conscious art with a capital *A* in the second—neatly encapsulates the experience of reading a Howe lyric. "Space is a frame we map ourselves in," Howe writes in the introduction. These lyrics, many of them the shapes of boxes (or paintings) make space and spatial arrangement their primary condition. Here is a passage from *Hinge Structure*:

> invisible angel confined
> to a point simpler than
> a soul a lunar sphere a
> demon darkened intelle
> ct mirror clear receiv
> ing the mute vocables
> of God that rained
> a demon daring down in h
> ieroglyph and stuttering

The above lines could have been written by any accomplished "experimental" poet of the last thirty years. Their indeterminacy, their conscious evasion of affect and style as those words are usually understood, their elevation of spatial constraints over formal ones, their rejection of the personal dimension, make them generic, and deliberately so. They exemplify the "dry disjunction" (as against "wet disjunction," the styles of Ashbery or Jorie Graham) that James Longenbach has identified as the signature of the avant-garde (*Resistance*). I have elsewhere traced the logics for this sort of poem and its deliberate elision of "individual" style. I wish merely to notice that style, or lack of style, in this poem.

Can a poem like the one I have quoted above be read with satisfaction if one carries into it expectations formed on the work of a Lowell or even an O'Hara? For whatever one does with it, what one does not and cannot do is read it like a self-sufficient artifact, teasing out its subtle implications. There is no "solving" a Howe lyric no matter how puzzle-like it may seem. Rather I think, we are meant to see "lyric" as one of several nested discourses in Howe's work. What matters is how much gets built on the "frame structures" of her early lyrics; what is surprising is how much of what gets built is autobiographical. The preface to *Frame Structures*, like Lowell's "91 Revere Street," seeks to render the unraveled remnants of the aristocracy, to see a culture under the sign of its own extinction. Poetry written under these conditions, no matter how abstract, will always be essentially narrative, and its success or failure seems to me to depend on its capacity to acknowledge narrative as a cause. Lowell's memoir and his memoir poems plough largely shared ground, and many of those poems began as prose reminiscences. Howe's memoir acts almost purely as a "frame," to add another meaning to that term: indeed she seems most interested in how certain kinds of frames create referential meaning in the artworks they surround, particularly where those artworks were, like the lyric above, entirely abstract.

But the fact that such a "frame" should be added long after the fact implies that, like the objects and notions Howe finds most seductive, poems age through time and, as they age, change their meanings, their meaningfulness. Howe loves the nearly comic displacements of objects through history, displacements traceable only because her family attained historical self-consciousness early on. For a Howe, having things means becoming an archivist of one's own life. Here is a representative paragraph: "The door to grandpa's apartment was in back where it was dark. Since the first floor was the second in terms of the complete living space, and living rooms in Louisburg Square had bay windows facing the street, his visitors must face the public gathering room by walking through the bedroom, and the first thing you saw in this intimate space, normally closed to the public in the genteel domestic arrangements of the 1940's, was a massive curtained double bed just like the Dore illustrations for 'Little Red Riding Hood.'" That bed—"the bed he was born in at Weetamoe" (the family's Rhode Island estate)—is elaborately framed, spatially by the curtain, by the bedroom door, by the windows of the house, and by the house itself and temporally by several acts of recollection that culminate in Howe's text. But it is, finally and at bottom, the bed Howe's grandfather was born in. An autobiographical fact as resonant as this would seem likely to be lost within its nested frames; instead, it is all the more vividly there.

A book like *Frame Structures* demonstrates how poetry makes selves (some of them abstract, or indeterminate, or symptomatic of dispersal) and how—far from proving the impossibility of self-integration—it shows its textual inevitability. Further, Howe's retrospective framing or reframing of her earliest poems implies a self continuous across time—an "author" in the strict old-fashioned sense. Similarly, Ron Silliman's *Under Albany* revisits early work in order to revise its context. The poem "Albany" (a mildly associative poem made up of one-hundred discreet sentences) serves now as a series of prompts for autobiographical recollection, recollection provided "under" the original line. Here is a typical entry, the line in bold print, the addendum below:

There is no such place as the economy, the self.

If a lion could speak, it would talk very slowly. Civilization constructed of complex nouns for which no exact equivalent in nature can be found. Identity is composed of our response, passionate or ambivalent, to exactly such muddy notations. Reading *Poetry Flash* with the photograph of Barrett looking boyish and introspective, I remember someone (Kit? Alan? Steve?) saying aloud, "It looks like we've been named."

Taking off from Wittgenstein's famous remark in the *Tractatus* ("If a lion could speak, we wouldn't understand him"), the "under" section tests the original hypothesis about the dynamic, rather than spatial and therefore fixed, machinery of selves (and "economies"). In one sense the susceptibility of people and groups of people to being known by their names ("Barrett" is of course Barrett Watten, and the "name" that "we" have been assigned is "the Language school") disproves the hypothesis. The place here is named *Poetry Flash* (crucially, another text) and the "self" is named "Barrett" or "Language school" (or elsewhere in this work, "Ron.") This entry is one of the least baldly autobiographical of the entire book, and still we see, alongside Wittgenstein and semiotics, untransformed "stuff" of an individual life at a fixed historical moment.

In both the Howe and the Silliman extracts, the retrospective act seems to occupy a wholly different semantic function from the original present-tense writing act. What would account for this discrepancy except for the fact that time has passed, experiences accumulated, identity, even if just by accident, been assigned? In Silliman the retrospective autobiography is tied, I believe, to his desire to deconstruct all self-authenticating monuments, to ruin what he calls "the Poem." This rhetoric, implicit in his newest work but also explicit at several moments in *Under Albany*, reminds one of nothing if not the turn away from and on the rather-too-tidy New Critical poem of the 1950s, the sort of poem Lowell's *Life Studies* has been pitched against. The analogy is surprisingly apt: both the "Language" lyric of the 1980s and the New Critical lyric of the 1950s were closed systems of linguistic moves, too dense for, and indeed ideologically opposed to, outside reference. Both lyrics came equipped with a kind of preexisting theoretical grid for understanding them, and both often seemed interested primarily in submitting to the forensic operations of critical procedure. Both lyrics had represented, it now seems, a kind of utopia of pure writing and pure reading. And both came to seem stifling (based on the evidence of Howe and Silliman) to their practitioners.

An additional cause of remorse for Language writers must be the appropriation of their ideas by the very cultural institutions and figures those ideas were meant to oppose. Vernon Shetley pointed out in 1993 how the various "aesthetic advantages" claimed on behalf of the Language school could be claimed, with equal merit, on behalf of MTV. And as the MTV vocabulary of diffuse, self-referential, and fragmentary signifiers has come to infect American habits of attention, nearly every aspect of American discourse has come to seem a lot more like a poem by Charles Bernstein than like one by Robert Lowell. "The proposed cure is distressingly similar to the symptoms of the disease," Shetley writes. Language poetry provided a brilliant mimesis of the structures of cognitive and linguistic attention, but once the mimesis was complete, capitalism went right on ticking. Interiority of the kind now allowed by Silliman and Howe and practiced all along by Lowell and Glück seems, in the present context of National Security Agency domestic spying, for example, a thing much threatened and therefore much to be prized.

Conclusion

The irony for any author whose primary theory of selfhood is based on dispersal is simply that those widely dispersed signs be finally collected and bound and shelved, his books read, his readers inspired, his poems commented on, his career the subject of still more books that are bound, shelved, read, and so on. This sense of having been defined, narrowly and much against one's will, is present in Silliman and Lowell both. Even for poets ideologically opposed to the self as an organizing term, the small assertions of continuity across time (revising my poems, collecting them, allowing books about them to be written) implies a person back there, behind them. And so the question of what constitutes a person, in poetic terms, and why persons matter to reading poems, becomes again an open one.

In *The Sighted Singer*, Allen Grossman makes a memorable distinction between persons and selves, arguing that it is the job of poetry to present the former—even, he suggests, by disregarding or disavowing the latter (Grossman 19). Poets find that "personhood and selfhood [are] in irreconcilable conflict," Grossman writes. "Poetry is anti-psychological."

In this last moment, I want to consider Grossman's distinction between persons and selves and his proposed relationship, or perhaps network of relationships, among poetry, selves, and persons. For it has been my claim throughout this book that poetry is most thoughtfully itself at this moment and in America when it brings self and person, to use Grossman's terms, into relation and when it does so within a full understanding of past renderings of self and person. His assumption, now ratified by twenty years of poetic practice (his own as well as others') that excessive attention to the conditions of selfhood might keep a poem from realizing personhood would seem to invalidate, in large part, all of the poetic projects I have discussed herein. Indeed (as I have said already) many of our most philosophically ambitious poets—Grossman among them—would consider autobiography to be at the very least an aesthetic dead end, and possibly an ethical one, as well.

What is a self, as distinct from a person? You might say that a self is a person minus a narrative. Grossman's sense of ontological personhood depends, it seems, on fragmentary presentations of self. We tend to associate lyric poetry with an uncanny clarity and nearness of voice, given historical estrangement. The anonymous lyric speakers of the Greek anthology, declaring, weirdly, across time, "I press her flesh. Our mouths are joined." Or the balladeers of early English tradition, singing, with terrific indignation, of the fates of ordinary people, or the first English lyric poets, all of them anonymous, celebrating the cuckoo's song or the arrival of night. There are sound theoretical reasons, based on the foundational stories of the lyric art, for connecting lyric poetry and anonymity: I am thinking of the renunciations of the social self (in grief, in religious devotion, in shame) described in the stories of Orpheus and, in Anglo-Saxon tradition, in Caedmon. For American poets, the lyric speaker's powerful renunciation of selfhood is renewed, and given political dimension, by Whitman, consolidated by the modernist poets of impersonality, and carried forward to the present day by poets of the Language school.

And yet in this book I have described an American poetry of excessive specificity and of fixed historical and cultural location. These persons have sometimes rather brutally qualified their ontological status—in Grossman's terms—by telling us so much about themselves. But these selves have often found viable lyric personhood by a surprising array of methods. From Lowell's poems of compromised sight, to Bishop's transparent masks, to O'Hara's renunciations of memory in favor of the radical present, to the experiments with voice, tone, and speakerly identity in Bidart and Glück, contemporary poems have brought tremendous pressure to bear on the representation of lived life.

My hope is that this book, far from framing the matter of autobiography historically and thereby locating it irretrievably in the past, opens it up again for fresh inspection. Our present poetic climate is wide open in terms of its interest in semantic indeterminacies, its love of far-flung idioms, and its omnivorous appetite for discourses of science and philosophy but very narrow in terms of possible stances toward the self, toward identity, and toward the weird category of experience we locate outside of language as "what happened." The Emersonian resonances of that term have not yet been fully sounded.

Works Cited

Abrams, M. H. *The Mirror and the Lamp*. New York: Oxford University Press, 1965.

Altieri, Charles. *Self and Sensibility in Modern Poetry*. New York: Cambridge University Press, 1984.

Anderson, Linda. *Autobiography*. New York and London: Routledge, 2001.

Bidart, Frank. *In the Western Night*. New York: Farrar, Straus & Giroux, 1990.

———. *Desire*. New York: Farrar, Straus & Giroux, 1997.

———. "Pre-existing Forms." Unpublished paper, 2000.

Bishop, Elizabeth. *The Complete Poems*. New York: Farrar, Straus & Giroux, 1989.

———. *One Art: Letters*. New York: Farrar, Straus & Giroux, 1994.

Blackmur, R. P. *The Double Agent*. New York: Arrow, 1935.

Blasing, Mutlu Konuk. *American Poetry: The Rhetoric of Its Forms*. New Haven, CT: Yale University Press, 1987.

Borges, Jorge Luis. *Borges: A Reader*. New York: E. P. Dutton, 1981.

Bromwich, David. *Skeptical Music*. Chicago: University of Chicago Press, 2001.

Browning, Robert. *The Oxford Authors*. New York: Oxford University Press, 1997.

Buell, Lawrence. *Emerson*. Cambridge, MA: Harvard University Press, Belknap Press, 2003.

Burr, Zofia, ed. *Set in Motion: Essays, Interviews, and Dialogues*, by
    A. R. Ammons. Ann Arbor: University of Michigan Press, 1999.

Burt, Stephen. "Poetry Criticism—What Is It For?" *Jacket*, vol. 11 (April
    2000). http://www.jacketmagazine.com/11/burt.html.

Cameron, Sharon. *Lyric Time*. Baltimore: Johns Hopkins University
    Press, 1979.

Costello, Bonnie. *Elizabeth Bishop: Questions of Mastery*. Cambridge,
    MA: Harvard University Press, 1991.

———. "*Meadowlands*: Trustworthy Speakers." In *On Louise
    Glück: Change What You See*, ed. Joanne Feit Diehl, 48–62. Under
    Discussion Series. Ann Arbor: University of Michigan Press, 2005.

Eliot, T. S. *The Complete Poems and Plays*. New York: Harcourt Brace,
    1952.

Emerson, Ralph Waldo. *Essays: Second Series*. Cambridge, MA:
    Belknap, 1983.

Encyclopædia Britannica Online. S.v. "Glück, Louise." http://search.eb.
    com/eb/article-9104307. (Accessed May 9, 2006.)

Ferguson, Margaret, Mary Jo Salter, and Jon Stallworthy, eds. *Norton
    Anthology of Poetry*. 4th ed. New York: Norton, 1996.

Ferry, David. *Eclogues of Virgil*. New York: Farrar, Straus & Giroux,
    1999.

Fisher, Philip. *Still the New World: American Literature in a Culture of
    Creative Destruction*. Cambridge, MA: Harvard University Press,
    1999.

Frost, Robert. *The Complete Poems*. New York: Library of America,
    1995.

Gardner, Helen. *The Composition of "Four Quartets."* New York: Oxford
    University Press, 1978.

Glück, Louise. *The Wild Iris*. Hopewell, NJ: Ecco, 1993.

———. *Proofs and Theories*. Hopewell, NJ: Ecco, 1994.

———. *The First Four Books of Poems*. Hopewell, NJ: Ecco, 1995.

———. *Meadowlands*. Hopewell, NJ: Ecco, 1996.

———. *Vita Nova*. New York: Ecco, 1999.

———. "Prism." In *Averno*. New York: Farrar, Straus & Giroux,
    2006.

Grossman, Allen. *The Sighted Singer: Two Works on Poetry for Writers
    and Readers*. Baltimore: Johns Hopkins University Press, 1992.

Halpern, Nick. *Everday and Prophetic*. Madison: University of
    Wisconsin Press, 2003.

Hass, Robert. "Poet's Choice." Review of *Vita Nova* by Louise Glück. *Washington Post*, August 8, 1999. Reprinted at http://www.english. uiuc.edu/maps/poets/g_l/gluck/about.htm.

Hejinian, Lyn. "The Person and Description." In "The Poetics of Everyday Life," ed. Barrett Watten and Lyn Hejinian, special issue, *Poetics Journal*, vol. 9 (1991). Quoted in Marjorie Perloff, "Language Poetry and the Lyric Subject: Ron Silliman's Albany, Susan Howe's Buffalo," *Critical Inquiry* 25, no. 3 (1999): 405.

Hofmann, Hans. *The Search for the Real*. Andover, MA: Addison Gallery of American Art, 1948.

Howe, Susan. *Frame Structures*. New York: New Directions, 1995.

Izenberg, Oren. "Language Poetry and Collective Life." *Critical Inquiry* 30, no. 1 (2003): 132–59.

Kalstone, David. *Becoming a Poet*. New York: Farrar, Straus & Giroux 1991.

Lehman, David. *The Last Avant-Garde*. New York: Anchor, 1999.

Longenbach, James. *Modern Poetry after Modernism*. New York: Oxford University Press, 1996.

———. *The Resistance to Poetry*. Chicago: University of Chicago Press, 2005.

Lowell, Robert. *Collected Poems of Robert Lowell*. New York: Farrar, Straus & Giroux, 2003.

Miller, Brett C. *Elizabeth Bishop: Life and the Memory of It*. Berkeley: University of California Press, 1995.

New, Elisa. *The Line's Eye*. Cambridge, MA: Harvard University Press, 1998.

O'Hara, Frank. *Autobiography: Essays Theoretical and Critical*. Princeton, NJ: Princeton University Press, 1980.

———. *Collected Poems*. Berkeley: University of California Press, 1995.

Ovid. *Metamorphoses*. Trans. Rolph Humphries. Bloomington: Indiana University Press, 1955.

Perloff, Marjorie. *The Dance of the Intellect*. Cambridge: Cambridge University Press, 1985.

———. *Frank O'Hara: Poet among Painters*. Austin: University of Texas Press, 1977.

———. "Language Poetry and the Lyric Subject: Ron Silliman's Albany, Susan Howe's Buffalo." *Critical Inquiry* 25, no. 3 (1999): 405–34.

Pinsky, Robert. *The Situation of Poetry.* Princeton, NJ: Princeton University Press 1976.

Pritchard, William. Review of *The Book of the Body*, by Frank Bidart.

Reynolds, David S. *Walt Whitman's America.* New York: Knopf, 1995.

Rich, Adrienne. "The Eye of the Outsider: The Poetry of Elizabeth Bishop." *Boston Review* 8 (April 1983): 17–19.

Schmidt, Dennis J. "Letter to Böhlendorf." App. C in *On Germans and Other Greeks: Tragedy and Ethical Life*, 165–67. Bloomington: Indiana University Press, 2001.

Shetley, Vernon. *After the Death of Poetry: Poet and Audience in Contemporary America.* Durham, NC: Duke University Press, 1993.

Silliman, Ron. *Under Albany.* London: Salt Press, 2005.

Solomon, Deborah. *Utopia Parkway: The Life and Work of Joseph Cornell.* New York: Farrar, Straus & Giroux, 1997.

Sontag, Kate, and David Graham, eds. *After Confession: Poetry as Autobiography.* Saint Paul, MN: Graywolf, 2001.

Stevens, Wallace. *The Collected Poems of Wallace Stevens.* New York: Vintage, 1982.

Stewart, Susan. *Poetry and the Fate of the Senses.* Chicago: University of Chicago Press, 2002.

Strand, Mark. *The Weather of Words.* New York: Alfred A. Knopf, 2000.

Vendler, Helen. *The Art of Shakespeare's Sonnets.* Cambridge, MA: Harvard University Press, 1997.

———. *Part of Nature, Part of Us.* Cambridge, MA: Harvard University Press, 1980.

Von Hallberg, Robert. *American Poetry and Culture, 1945–1980.* Cambridge, MA: Harvard University Press, 1985.

Whitman, Walt. *Leaves of Grass: A Norton Critical Edition.* New York: Norton, 1973.

Williamson, Alan. *Introspection and Contemporary Poetry.* Cambridge, MA: Harvard University Press, 1984.

———. *Pity the Monsters: The Political Vision of Robert Lowell.* New Haven, CT: Yale University Press, 1974.

Yeats, William Butler. *Collected Poems of William Butler Yeats.* New York: Macmillan: 1933.

———. *Essays and Introductions.* New York: Macmillan, 1968.

Index